New, Expanded Edition

All-Maine Seafood Cookbook

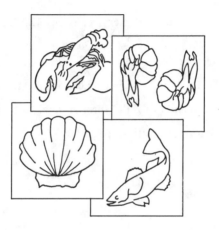

Compiled and Edited by Loana Shibles and

Annie Rogers, with New Recipes Compiled by

Raquel Boehmer

Illustrations by James Kingsland

DOWN EAST B(

D0596013

Acknowledgements

Thanks are extended especially to National Marine Fisheries Service, Chicago, and the Maine Department of Sea & Shore Fisheries, Augusta, for their interest, and to the following for the use of photographs.

National Marine Fisheries Service, pages 12, 42, 65, 80, 90, 98, 114, 119, 131, 153, 165

Copley News Service, pages 16, 57, 126

Lewis/Neale, Inc. for J. Walter Thompson, page 142

Best Foods, Division of CPC International, Inc., page 160

American Dairy Association, page 178

Section Reference

"Good cooks are born, not made, they say.
The saying is untrue;
Hard trying and these recipes
Will make a good cook of you."

—*copied from an old, old cookbook*

Introduction

Fishing has been an established part of the State of Maine's activity for over 400 years and nearly 300 fishing vessels from four European countries were reported off these shores as far back as the 16th century.

In 1604, Champlain met a fisherman in Penobscot Bay who said he had made 42 lobstering trips from Europe to Maine.

A year later, Capt. George Waymouth and his crew aboard the "Archangel" visited the island of Monhegan, ten miles offshore from Port Clyde, and found the fishing "excellent."

"While we were on shore our men aboard with a few hooks got about thirty great cods and haddocks which gave us a taste of the great plenty of fish which we found afterward wheresoever we went upon the coast," his chronicler, James Rosier, reported.

Capt. John Smith also found the fish in Monhegan waters to be both plentiful and good. While he and his men mended their gear at a crescent-shaped beach on the island in 1614, he observed, "What pleasure can be more than to recreate themselves before their own doors in their own boats upon the sea where man, woman, and child, with a small hook and line, by angling, may take diverse sorts of excellent fish at their pleasure!"

Freshwater fish from Maine's thousands of streams, lakes, and ponds have always been a staple.

Over the centuries, Maine's good fish have attracted many visitors to explore, and to fish for profit or pleasure.

Rockland is the state's leading port in fish landings, of nearly 60 million pounds yearly, valued at $8,000,000, and is the leading port for assembly and shipping of the fish and shellfish. It is also the site of the Maine Seafoods Festival each August, where visitors from far and near sample the good fish of Maine.

We hope this cookbook, with recipes garnered from Maine cooks the length and breadth of the state, will help you prepare Maine's good fish in old and new ways for your enjoyment and that of your family.

Loana Shibles
Annie Rogers

From the Islands of Maine

by Raquel Boehmer

Seafood is in! That's the new cry in food circles. All over, people from every walk of life have discovered the healthfulness of fin and shellfish. As a result, consumption of seafoods in the United States is going up—14.5 pounds per person in 1985 (almost 1½ lb. more than 1983), according to the National Marine Fisheries Service, and gaining yearly. This is not surprising when you couple a national concern for improved fitness and health with the low fat, high protein content of seafoods. Besides, the generally quick cooking feature of seafoods makes them convenient choices for busy working people.

This is good news, but it also presents a problem: increased demand has resulted in overfishing, causing shortages and threatening certain stocks of favored fish. At the same time, good catches of less familiar (although delicious) fish, such as pollock, hake, cusk, and whiting, are not being sought out by shoppers. These fish are all in the same family as cod and haddock, and they deserve our attention. Generally, the recipes for all members of the cod family are interchangeable.

Other underutilized but abundant Maine species, including mussels, mackerel, and squid, meet with new devotees wherever they are introduced via markets and restaurants. Good recipes for these seafoods can only help encourage people to try them.

When considering this revised edition of *All Maine Seafood*, I thought it logical to take up the participatory spirit begun by Loana Shibles and Annie Rogers by just expanding the contributions to include a new chapter exclusively from island folks. In addition, this new section would focus on the interchangeability of less familiar species. This is exactly what's been done!

On many of the islands of Maine, preparing and serving meals is a central part of evenings spent with friends. Even on the bigger islands, after the summer season there are few, if any, restaurants to pick from. As a result, the islanders, both male and female, are great cooks.

In these pages you will find seafood recipes from their list of favorites. On an island you often have to make do with what's available, and the concept of interchangeability is a natural development of simply using whatever is the freshest of what is on hand. Two fishermen have added some information on wolf fish (ocean cat) and a way of preparing salt mackerel. In keeping with current food trends, there are quiche recipes and two offerings that call for surimi (imitation crabmeat that offers a large future market for Maine's abundant hake and whiting). Picked crabmeat from Maine's rock crabs is a special favorite among islanders. These crustaceans are an incidental catch; they come up in the deep-water lobster traps.

I am especially grateful for the valuable help provided by the Rev. Stan Haskell, who served the Maine Sea Coast Mission aboard the MV *Sunbeam*, and to Philip Conkling of the Island Institute. To the original editors, I extend praise for their marvelous concept and endeavor. But above all, thanks go to the generous folks who shared their island recipes. May all who read this book enjoy the varied fruits of the sea.

Mother's Modifiable Fish Loaf

¾ cup hot milk
2 cups soft bread crumbs—
no crust
2 cups fish, cooked, any kind
(I use pollock)
2 eggs, beaten
Pepper
2 tablespoons celery, chopped
2 tablespoons parsley, chopped

2 tablespoons green pepper,
chopped
2 tablespoons onion, chopped
1 teaspoon salt
1 cup coarsely mashed,
cooked carrots, or any mild
cooked vegetable (such as
peas or green beans)

[Cod, haddock, salmon, hake, cusk, or whiting all work well in this recipe.]

Note: If you have onion haters in the family, serve onions on the side.

Mix together first five ingredients. Add remaining items and place mixture in a bread pan. Bake in 375 degree oven for about 45 minutes till the loaf tests done.

Submitted by Jean Dyer, Chebeague Island, Maine

Seafood Quiche

9- or 10-inch unbaked pie or
quiche shell
1½ cups milk or cream
1¼ cups cheese, grated
1 teaspoon onion, grated

1 tablespoon green pepper,
finely minced
3 eggs, beaten
Salt and pepper to taste
1 pound seafood: crab, lobster,
shrimp, or a combination

Scald milk or cream. Add grated cheese and stir until melted. Then add in the remaining ingredients. Place all in the prepared pie or quiche shell. Bake at 350 degrees for 45 minutes or until firm.

Submitted by Shirley Brown, North Haven Island, Maine

Fish Turbet

Boil 3 cups haddock (any white fish such as hake, cusk, cod, or pollock may be substituted). Save ½ cup of the fish water for sauce.

Sauce Ingredients:

¼ cup butter or margarine
Half a green pepper, chopped
¼ cup onion, finely minced
2 tablespoons flour
½ cup milk
½ cup reserved fish water
  (see above)

¼ pound shredded cheddar
  cheese
½ teaspoon lemon juice
½ teaspoon salt
¼ teaspoon pepper

Buttered bread crumbs
Pimento strips

Melt butter, and saute green pepper and onion in it until soft. Add flour, stir, and add the milk and broth. Continue to stir until mixture is smooth and thickened. Add the shredded cheese, stir to melt, and then add the remaining sauce ingredients. Arrange the cooked fish in the bottom of a buttered casserole. Cover with the sauce and top with buttered bread crumbs and pimento strips. Bake in 350 degree oven until top is brown. This is an old recipe from a generation ago.

Submitted by Hazel Skillings, Peaks Island, Maine

Creamy Fish Chowder

2 or 3 large white potatoes
1 or 2 large onions
Water
1 teaspoon salt
½ teaspoon pepper
1½ to 2 pounds firm white
  fish fillets (cod, cusk,
  pollock, etc.)

2 cups milk
½ cup butter or margarine
  (1 stick)
8 slices processed American
  cheese

Peel and cube potatoes (¾" pieces). Coarsely chop onions. In a large covered pot, boil onions and potatoes in enough water to not quite cover. Add salt and pepper. Wash fish and cut it into ¾" cubes. When the vegetables are *almost* cooked, add fish and enough water to cover the fish. Reduce heat and simmer about ½ hour. Over a very low heat, stir in milk and butter. Return to a slow boil. Once boiling, add cheese, stirring occasionally until the cheese melts. Adjust seasonings. Serve piping hot, with crackers. Serves four nicely.

Submitted by Brian Hubbard, U.S. Coast Guard,
Manana Island, Maine

Shellfish in Crispy Batter

1 cup flour
2 tablespoons baking powder
1¼ teaspoons salt
2 teaspoons sugar

1 tablespoon cooking oil
1 cup water
½ cup shrimp, mussel meats,
  or picked lobster meat

Combine flour, baking powder, salt and sugar. Add vegetable oil to water. Make a well in dry ingredients and very slowly pour in combined liquids. Stir till well blended. Allow to set 10 minutes. Heat deep-frying oil to 375 degrees F. Dip shellfish in batter and deep-fry 3 to 4 minutes, till golden. Drain well on paper towels. Serve with tartar sauce or lemon wedges.

Submitted by Beverly Jones, Long Island, Maine

Smoked Mussels

Steam enough mussels to fill your smoker and remove meats from shells. Prepare enough brine to cover the meats in a glass, pottery, or plastic container.

Brine: To each cup of water, add one cup salt, 2 tablespoons dark brown sugar, 2 tablespoons lemon juice, 1 tablespoon Worcestershire sauce, 1 large onion (chopped), and 2 minced cloves of garlic.

Soak the meats one hour in the brine and drain. Rinse in cool water and lay mussels on wire rack or screen to air dry for 1½ to 2 hours. While the mussels are drying, warm the smoker and start the smoking process with chips of hickory (my preference), apple, maple, alder, or other hardwood. Smoke about one hour. Remove from smoker and put in large jar, adding ½ cup olive or other oil. Place jar on its side and rotate occasionally so mussels absorb oil. Add more oil if you wish. When cool, refrigerate or freeze.

Submitted by Alice A. Kelleter, Vinalhaven, Maine

Stuffed Mussels

2 dozen mussels
½ cup bread crumbs
¼ cup butter, melted

1 tablespoon onion, chopped
1 teaspoon dill weed

Steam the mussels in small amount of water. Pick out the meats, saving the shells and reserving some broth. Grind the mussel meats. Add the other ingredients and enough mussel broth to moisten to a workable consistency. Spoon into mussel shell halves. Broil for 5 to 10 minutes.

Submitted by Elsie Gillespie, Swan's Island, Maine

Mussels Gratin

2 tablespoons margarine	½ teaspoon salt
1 onion, chopped	Pepper
1 clove garlic, minced	Nutmeg
2 cups mussel meats, steamed	2 to 4 ounces Swiss cheese,
3 eggs, whites and yolks	shredded
beaten separately	¼ cup sherry
1½ cups milk	Butter or margarine

In heated margarine, cook the onion and garlic slightly. Add mussel meats and fold all together with the other ingredients. Put into deep baking dish, dot butter or margarine on top. Bake at 350 degrees about 40 minutes until lightly browned and a little firm. Serve immediately.

Mussels are so good in many well known dishes, taking the place of meat or fish. Try them in casseroles, quiche, stuffed zucchini, stuffed eggplant, shepherd's pie, chowder, and pizza!

Submitted by Rosamond Lord, Islesford, Maine

Steamed Mussels

4 dozen mussels, well scrubbed	½ teaspoon thyme, or 2 fresh
½ cup white wine	sprigs
2 shallots or scallions, chopped	4 dried bay leaves

Place all in a large kettle and over high heat, bring to a boil. Cover and steam for about 20 minutes. Liquor may be thickened slightly with a flour and water paste or served as is. Sop it up with crusty French bread.

Georgie Ware, Cranberry Isles, Maine

Cousin Ted's Scallop Casserole

1 pound scallops
1½ cups stale bread cubes
1 cup cheddar cheese, grated
Salt and pepper to taste

½ cup medium cream
3 tablespoons sherry
  (or orange juice)
Butter

Wash scallops and cut them up if they are large. Toss together with bread cubes, cheddar cheese, salt, and pepper. Put in buttered casserole dish. Mix cream with the sherry or orange juice, and pour over the scallop mixture. Dot with butter and bake at 350 degrees for ½ hour, or until browned.

Submitted by Elsie Rice, North Haven Island, Maine

Marinated Scallops

1 pound scallops, quartered
½ cup red onions, sliced
¾ cup lime juice
3 tablespoons oil
2 tablespoons white wine
½ teaspoon ground coriander
Tabasco sauce—a dash

1 tablespoon green jalapeno
  pepper, chopped—fresh
  or canned
1 teaspoon salt
½ teaspoon pepper
⅛ teaspoon basil
¼ cup chopped parsley

Note: mild green bell pepper may be substituted for the hot chili pepper.

Combine all ingredients in a non-corrosive bowl or glass jar. Place in refrigerator and marinate for 24 hours. (The citric acid in the lime juice "cold cooks" the scallops by an enzymatic action.)

Submitted by Shirley Brown, North Haven Island, Maine

Scalloped Scallops a la Castine

1 pound scallops
¼ cup butter or oleo
16 Ritz crackers, crushed

½ cup cream or evaporated
  milk
2 tablespoons sherry
Salt and pepper to taste

In a shallow greased baking dish, arrange fresh scallops, cut large-grape size, in one layer only. Melt butter, add crushed cracker crumbs and sprinkle about half of this mixture over scallops, working crumbs around scallops. Over this, pour cream and sherry. Add salt and pepper to taste. (The liquid should barely cover scallops.) Top with remaining buttered crumbs. Bake ½ hour at 350 degrees.

Submitted by Connie Pierce, North Haven Island, Maine

Cream Crab

1 quart milk
Piece of butter or margarine
   size of walnut

½ cup flour stirred with water
   enough to make a paste
Crabmeat, 1 pound or more
Salt and pepper to taste

Make a white sauce by combining the milk, butter, and flour paste and stirring (on low heat) till thickened and smooth. Then add the crabmeat and seasonings, stirring just until the mixture begins to bubble. To give more flavor to it, you can make this in the morning if you want a light supper, or the day before if you'd like it at noon, and store it, covered, in the refrigerator.

Submitted by Rebecca Lunt, Frenchboro Island, Maine

Crab Casserole

2 cups elbow macaroni
3 tablespoons butter
3 tablespoons flour
1 teaspoon salt
½ teaspoon dry mustard
1½ cups milk

1 cup sour cream
3 tablespoons minced onion
1 cup sharp cheese, grated
2 cups crabmeat
3 tablespoons dry seasoned
   bread crumbs

Cook and drain macaroni. Melt butter, stir in flour and seasonings. Slowly add milk and stir over medium heat until thickened. Remove from heat, fold in sour cream, onion and cheese. Add crabmeat and macaroni. Stir all together. Put bread crumbs on top. Bake at 325 degrees for 20 to 30 minutes.

Submitted by Elizabeth Anderson Prior, Ragged Island, Maine

Crab Strata

6 eggs
3 cups milk
1½ teaspoons mustard
¾ teaspoon onion powder
¾ teaspoon salt
Pepper to taste
⅓ cup butter, melted

2 tablespoons flour
¾ cup sliced almonds
8 slices white bread, crusts removed
1 pound crabmeat
¾ pound shredded Swiss cheese

Beat eggs, add milk, mustard, onion powder, salt and pepper, melted butter, and flour. Toast almonds in 350 degree oven for 15 minutes. Line a buttered 3-quart dish with four of the slices of bread that have been cut into 6 squares each. Layer half the crabmeat, half the cheese, half the almonds, and repeat, finishing with the almonds. Top with 1-inch bread cubes cut from remaining bread slices. This preparation can be done ahead and all refrigerated until ready to cook. At that time, pour egg mixture over the layered ingredients. Bake at 350 degrees for 50 to 60 minutes or until an inserted knife comes out clean. Serves 8.

Submitted by Robertine Gray, Cranberry Isles, Maine

Crab Quiche

9-inch partially baked pie shell (5 minutes at 350 degrees)
2 tablespoons minced onion
2 tablespoons margarine
3-ounce can sliced mushrooms, drained (save broth)
4 eggs, beaten
¾ cup light cream

½ teaspoon salt
Dash of cayenne
⅛ teaspoon tarragon
¼ teaspoon marjoram
Dash of pepper
½ pound crabmeat
½ cup Swiss cheese, grated

Saute onion in the margarine until tender. Add all but 10 slices of mushrooms and continue to saute until hot. In a separate bowl, combine beaten eggs, light cream, mushroom broth, and spices. Fold in sauteed onion and mushrooms and then the crabmeat. Pour into pie shell, sprinkle with cheese, and top with the reserved mushrooms. Bake in 350 degree oven for 35 minutes or until golden brown. Let stand 5 minutes before serving.

Submitted by Barbara Smith, Cliff Island, Maine

Josie Conary's Salad Dressing for Lobster Salad

2 level teaspoons dry mustard
½ cup sugar
1 egg, beaten
½ cup vinegar
½ cup milk

2 level teaspoons flour
Butter, size of walnut
Water
Sprinkling of pepper

In top half of a double boiler, over boiling water, mix together the first four ingredients. Then slowly add milk. Lastly, mix the flour with enough water to make a paste that's not too watery, and add to the mixture in double boiler. Continue to cook until a bit thickened (will thicken more while cooling). Add the piece of butter and sprinkle with pepper. Makes about 2 cups.

Submitted by Josephine Swann, Swan's Island, Maine

Lobster Quiche

9-inch unbaked pastry shell
1 cup lobster meat, cooked
1 cup cheddar cheese,
   shredded
½ cup onion, minced

4 eggs, beaten
2 cups light cream
½ teaspoon salt
¼ teaspoon cayenne pepper
Dash of parsley flakes

Preheat oven to 425 degrees. Sprinkle lobster, cheese, and onion into shell. Pour cream into eggs and add seasonings and parsley flakes. Pour into shell. Bake for 15 minutes at 425 degrees, then reduce heat to 300 degrees. Bake 35 to 45 minutes or until knife comes out clean when inserted 1 inch from edge. Let quiche stand for 10 minutes before serving.

Submitted by Muriel Anderson, Cliff Island, Maine

Squid in Tomato Sauce

To clean squid: Hold tentacles in one hand and body in the other. Pull firmly and the tentacles will separate. Place tentacles on a board, cut just beyond the fleshy bulbous part and save the tentacles while discarding the rest. The body part (sac) has a quill (qualifying it for the shellfish family) which you can feel with your fingers. Pull the quill out and discard it. Flush body under cold running water while gently rubbing off the speckled outer skin.

Rinse saved tentacles and body in several changes of cold water. Slice body open and cut into approximately 2-inch squares. Chop the tentacles into 1-inch pieces. Proceed with any chosen recipe. Note: the body can be sliced into rings, if desired.

4 tablespoons olive oil
2 or 3 garlic cloves, minced or pressed
2 medium onions, sliced
¼ cup celery, chopped
¼ cup green pepper, chopped
2 pounds squid, cleaned and cut up as described above

1 (16 oz) can tomatoes, drained and chopped (save liquid)
1 (6 oz) can tomato paste
Red wine, a splash
Salt and pepper, as desired
Cooked pasta (linguine or spaghetti)
Parsley, chopped, fresh or dried

Heat oil in skillet or saucepan on low heat. Add garlic, onion, celery, and green pepper and slowly saute until onion slices are limp. Then saute squid pieces for only two minutes. Put drained tomatoes and tomato paste in saucepan. Add a canful (paste size) of the saved tomato liquid and a splash of red wine. Stir. Cover and simmer gently for 20 to 30 minutes.

Meanwhile, prepare the pasta. Check squid and tomato sauce for salt and pepper, seasoning as desired. When pasta is ready, pour sauce over each serving. Top with parsley. This can be prepared a day or two ahead and refrigerated. Serves 4 to 6.

Raquel Boehmer, Monhegan Island, Maine

Eggs Periwinkle

1½ cups shelled periwinkle meats (or as many as you have the endurance and help to pick out)

6 eggs
2 tablespoons butter
1 cup thick Roque Island cream (or any heavy cream)
toast

Collect periwinkles (and/or whelks, for variety) at extreme low tide, selecting the largest ones. Boil for a few minutes in salted water. As soon as the opercula, or limy doors, drop off and the animals protrude, remove from boiling water. Using a pin or nut-pick, twist each morsel from its spiral shell (retain the juice as much as possible). While poaching the 6 eggs, melt butter in frying pan and saute periwinkle meats for about two minutes. Add cream and periwinkle liquid and reduce, stirring until thickened. Pour over eggs, on toast. Serves 6.

Submitted by Anita Herrick Keams and Katryna Brett Herrick,
Roque Island, Maine

Oriental Cusk

1½ to 2 pounds cusk fillets,
   cut into about 1-inch pieces

Marinade:
2 tablespoons soy sauce
1 garlic clove, minced
Fresh ginger, grated

Tempura batter:
½ cup flour
½ cup cornstarch
½ teaspoon salt
1 egg, separated
½ cup water

Stir to coat fish pieces with marinade and let stand ½ hour. Sift dry batter ingredients together. Beat egg yolks and add water, then dry ingredients, stirring lightly. Beat egg whites until stiff but not dry and fold into batter.

Remove fish from marinade, drain, and dip in batter. Fry in hot oil 1 inch deep until fish is golden and tests done. Hold cooked fish in warm oven (200 degrees) while preparing remainder.

Stir fry: Cut up and stir fry your favorite oriental vegetable mixture. (Example: onion, green pepper, celery, garlic, and carrots.) Cook them only until crisp-tender. Now add 1 cup water with 1 chicken bouillon cube (or broth) and grated fresh ginger to taste. When this liquid comes to a simmer, stir in a paste you have made from ½ cup water and 2 teaspoons cornstarch. Stir this into the cooked vegetables and broth until the liquid is thickened. Then add 2 tablespoons soy sauce and a pinch of sugar. Lift out the cooked vegetables to a large serving platter, pile fish on top, and pour remaining liquid from the stir fry over the fish. Serve with rice. Makes 8 generous servings.

[Note: monkfish or wolf fish may be substituted for cusk.]

Submitted by Barbara F. Stanley, Monhegan Island, Maine

Haddock and "Rat Cheese" Casserole

1 tablespoon butter or
  margarine
1 tablespoon flour
1 cup milk
½ teaspoon salt

½ teaspoon mustard
⅛ teaspoon pepper
1 cup shredded very sharp
  cheddar (rat) cheese
1½ pounds haddock fillets

Arrange fish in buttered casserole. Make a white sauce of butter, flour, milk, salt, mustard, and pepper. When sauce is smooth and thick, mix in cheese. Stir until cheese is melted. Pour sauce over fish and bake at 350 degrees for 45 minutes, or until fish separates when tested with a fork. You can use lobster, scallops, and crabmeat, or a combination of these, in the casserole.

[Note: Cod, pollock, hake, whiting, or cusk could also be substituted for the haddock.]

Submitted by Ruth S. Stanley, Cranberry Isles, Maine

Baked Haddock with Sour Cream

1 pound fresh haddock
1 cup dairy sour cream
1 teaspoon lemon juice
2 teaspoons Maine maple
  syrup

4 tablespoons cornflake or
  bread crumbs
Seasoned salt or paprika

Arrange haddock on foil in a greased baking dish. Mix the sour cream, lemon juice, and maple syrup. Spread sour cream mixture on fish and top with crumbs and seasonings. Bake in hot oven (425 degrees) for about 35 minutes.

[Note: Cod, pollock, cusk, hake, or whiting may be substituted for the haddock.]

Submitted by Elizabeth Anderson Prior,
Ragged Island, Maine

Grandma Lenfesty's Salmon Loaf

2 eggs
⅓ cup milk
1 can salmon, drained and
  deboned. Save the liquid.
½ teaspoon celery salt
⅔ cup poultry stuffing
  (Pepperidge Farm Cornbread
  Stuffing recommended)

1 medium onion, sliced

Cream (white) sauce:
4 tablespoons margarine or
  butter
4 tablespoons flour
2 cups milk
½ teaspoon salt
Pepper to taste

In a bowl, beat eggs, add milk, liquid from the salmon, and celery salt. Mix in the stuffing and fold in salmon. Add onion. Place mixture in a 5 x 7-inch bread pan. Cover pan very loosely with foil and set in a larger pan with water to a 1-inch depth to prevent burning on bottom. Bake about 1 hour, checking at 45 minutes by inserting a knife to see if it comes out clean. When done, loosen around the edges, invert onto a serving plate, accompanied by the cream sauce to be poured over servings.

Submitted by Ronald H. Peabody, U.S. Coast Guard,
Manana Island, Maine

Grilled Shark Steak

1 lb. shark steak (mackerel
  or mako, for example)
  cut into 1″ slices

Marinade:
⅓ cup soy sauce
3 tablespoons salad oil
1 teaspoon dry mustard
½ teaspoon grated fresh ginger
¼ teaspoon pepper
1 clove garlic, minced

Marinate sliced shark in the above mixture for ½ hour. Grill on barbeque or broil in the oven. Do not overcook; count on 10 minutes per inch thickness. Also good pan-fried in butter.

Submitted by Barbara F. Stanley, Monhegan Island, Maine

Boiled Salt Mackerel

While salting down fresh bait for a trip out tub trawling, pick out one fine fresh mackerel for each man in your crew. Split each (fish) down the back, wash in salt water, and liberally sprinkle with salt, placing fish skin-side down on a board. When your gear is set, the boat anchored up, and the crew is settled down, put a kettle of peeled Maine potatoes and several large onions on to boil. In the meantime, again rinse your mackerel, taking notice of their splendid color. When the potatoes are nearly done, hove in the mackerel and let them cook until they will flake apart.

A little butter and pepper on the potatoes and a bottle of beer will make the whole works go down nicely, as well as to provide the extra energy you'll need to wrestle a big old halibut over the side shortly after daylight!

Note: Mackerel can be prepared in this fashion, at home, too!
Submitted by Capt. Lexi Krause, Monhegan Island, Maine

Wolf Fish (Ocean Catfish)

I like to fillet the fish right aboard the boat while it's fresh. I dry the fillets with a paper towel; I never wash fish if it can be avoided.

To prepare for cooking, spread fillets with butter and sprinkle with salt and pepper and a pinch of tarragon. Place them on foil on a shallow broiler pan and broil until white halfway through (about 5 minutes for 1-inch-thick fillet). Flip over carefully and place more butter on top. This keeps it from drying out. Cook till white all the way through—*not more!* When done, squeeze a little lemon juice over fish and serve.

To charcoal grill, I like a low fire. Don't let flames char the fish. To insure this, use foil under the fillets in order to catch the drippings so that they will not cause the coals to flare up. I butter the fillets the same way as above, and cover tent them loosely with foil. This retains smoky flavor and keeps them moist.

Wolf fish is one of our best eating fish. Its flesh is firm and I rate it with halibut. These instructions work for cusk also.
Submitted by Jay Speakman, Islesford, Maine

Surimi Hoppin' John

Surimi offers great hope to the fisheries because it is made from some less-favored species. The state of Maine requires that it be strictly and clearly labeled to distinguish it from genuine crab, scallop, shrimp, or lobster meat. Be sure to read the label if you have allergies to certain salts and flavorants; some brands do not include additives.

½ pound surimi (imitation crab), flaked, salad-style
1 cup black-eyed peas, cooked
1 cup rice (white or brown), cooked
2 tablespoons yogurt

2 tablespoons mayonnaise
¼ teaspoon curry powder (optional)
¼ cup scallions, finely chopped, including 2 inches of green tops

This dish can be mixed while peas and rice are hot, and the Hoppin' John served right away while it is warm. Or, you can chill the mixture and then serve it as a salad, over greens.

Blend the surimi with the black-eyed peas and rice, tossing gently. Combine yogurt, mayonnaise and curry powder in a separate bowl, then stir into the surimi mixture with care. Whether serving this dish hot or cold, top with chopped scallions.

Raquel Boehmer, Monhegan Island, Maine

Surimi Salad

½ pound surimi (imitation crabmeat), salad style, shredded
1 cup fresh (or frozen) green beans, cooked, cut

¼ cup celery, finely cut
¼ cup yogurt
¼ cup mayonnaise

Cut up the surimi a little finer than it comes from the store and place in a bowl. Add the prepared vegetables, which will support the delicate flavor of the surimi. Mix the yogurt and mayonnaise together and stir into the assembled ingredients. This will make four adequate servings of the salad.

Submitted by Gretchen Hall, Peaks Island, Maine

Shellfish

Fish and shellfish are nutritious. They are valuable sources of animal protein, minerals and essential vitamins. Compared to other complete protein foods, the fat content of fish is low.

The flavor, texture and appearance of the fish and shellfish vary according to their species but the fundamental rules for cooking seafoods are few and easy to follow.

All seafoods may be cooked by any of the basic cooking methods, such as frying, baking, broiling, boiling or steaming and in an endless variety of combination dishes. The most important thing to remember in cooking fish is that it is too often overcooked. Just enough cooking to enable the fish to be flaked easily when tested with a fork will leave the fish moist, tender and bring out its delicate flavor.

The commercial catch of fish and shellfish landed at ports on the Atlantic coast amounts to about 50% of the U. S. total catch.

Some 16,457,666 pounds of lobsters were landed in Maine in 1974 representing a value of $23,212,808, and 9,770,732 pounds of saltwater shrimp, for a value of $3,465,764.

Other shellfish brought into Maine ports and harbors in sizable quantities are clams, of course, rock crabs, scallops and some oysters. Growing quantities of mussels, periwinkles and squid are also being brought ashore to meet a growing demand for these delicacies.

Angels On Horseback
(This recipe came from a coastal fisherman in his language.)

"Take the shell, clean it, put the clam in, then a very little red pepper, then grate an onion, put in a little, cover the clam with bacon. These are in a baker pan, of course. Put in oven and when the bacon is cooked, the clam is."

It's a mighty good recipe.

Submitted by Josephine C. Philbrick, Camden, Maine

Clam Pie

Favorite pie crust for two-crust pie, only rolled thicker
3 potatoes
1 quart soft clams
4 ounces salt pork
1 small onion
1 tablespoon flour

Boil potatoes in their skins until almost tender, peel and cube. Wash and grind clams, save juice and some bellies. Cube salt pork and cook slowly until golden brown, add onion. Stir in flour, then potatoes and clams. Mix ingredients. Pour in pie dough in 9-inch pie plate. Put top crust on. Seal and bake in 425 degree oven 20 minutes then in 350 degree oven 25 minutes.

Submitted by Mrs. Dolores Reglin, Orrington, Maine

Clams With Cream

50 small clams
Pepper
Salt
Butter (size of egg)
1 teaspoon flour
1 cup cream (heated to boiling)

Chop the clams (save the liquor) and season with pepper and salt. Put the butter in a stew pan and heat until it bubbles. Sprinkle in the flour and cook a few minutes. Gradually stir into it the clam liquor then the clams and stew about 2 or 3 more minutes. Add the boiling cream and serve immediately.

Submitted by L. G. Tennies, Westport Island, Wiscasset, Maine

Leftover Steamed Clams Elegante

I usually steam all the clams my husband brings home from a clamming trip. After the first meal of steamers I pick out the remaining clams, save the biggest and best shells which I wash and clean and set outside to bleach.

With the meats picked out, I carefully clean the meats, letting them set overnight in refrigerator in clam broth makes this simple, as the sand in the rims will drop off in the broth and they will be sand-free the next day. Cut off the necks, remove black from bellies and chop finely, either in wooden bowl with hand chopper or through the meat grinder.

Take about six strips of bacon and fry out, drain slices on paper towels. Leave grease in fry pan, chop bacon slices to fine pieces. Peel and chop one medium onion fine, fry to transparency in remaining bacon fat.

Take chopped clams, chopped bacon, cooked onion and mix in bowl with about 6 eight-inch "milk crackers" which are finely crumbled. This seems to blend and taste better than with salted crackers. Add seasoning to taste, such as Worcestershire sauce, Tabasco, etc.

Grease bleached shells well, fill with this mixture and top with some crushed salted crackers lightly sauteed in butter. Place in low oven to heat thoroughly. Oven cannot be over 300 degrees as shells tend to crack in higher oven.

This is a delightful cocktail party specialty, or good on any occasion and I have had many requests for this recipe. These can be made ahead and placed in freezer. Take out shortly before use and put into oven for final cooking.

Submitted by Mrs. Donald Stewart, Castine, Maine

Backyard Clambake

12 small onions	12 pieces of cheesecloth
6 medium size potatoes	(18" x 36" each)
6 ears corn in husks	12 pieces heavy duty foil
6 dozen steamer clams	(18" x 36" each)
6 live lobsters (1 pound each)	

(1) Start fire about 25 minutes ahead so coals will be hot.

(2) Peel onions and wash potatoes, parboil onions and potatoes for 15 minutes, drain.

5   continued

(3) Remove corn silk from corn and pull husks back in place. Wash clam shells thoroughly.

(4) Place 2 pieces of cheesecloth on top of 2 pieces of foil. Place 2 onions, 1 potato, 1 ear of corn, 1 lobster and 1 dozen clams on cheesecloth. Tie opposite corners of cheesecloth together. Pour 1 cup water over food and bring foil up over the package and close all edges with tight double folds. Repeat five times until you have 6 packages.

(5) Place packages on grill about 4 inches from hot coals. Cover with hood or aluminum foil. Cook for 45 to 60 minutes or until potatoes and onions are tender. Serve with melted butter. Makes 6 servings.

Submitted by Lulu M. Miller, Waldoboro, Maine

Mother's Clam Pie

Use an 8-inch pie plate: Make regular pie crust for a two-crust pie. Roll out half of dough for the bottom crust. Take a pint of clams, chop the hard part and mix with the soft part. Stir in a little flour and clam liquid and pour into pie shell. Sprinkle with salt and pepper and dot with butter. Cover with top crust and bake in 375 degree oven for 1 hour or until crust is browned.

Submitted by Clara W. Thornton, North Haven, Maine

Clamburgers

1 pint clams (chopped fine)
1 cup cracker crumbs
1 egg, well beaten

1 teaspoon salt
¼ teaspoon pepper

Mix well, form into round cakes and fry in hot fat, about 1 inch deep. Drain on paper and serve.

Submitted by Goldie Chadwick, Thomaston, Maine

State Of Maine Clam Chowder

1 quart fresh shucked Maine clams
Liquor from clams
1 quart diced Maine potatoes, uncooked

1 onion, diced
1 quart milk, scalded
2 tablespoons margarine
Salt to taste (add at end)

Remove black vein parts and windpipes from clams, saving liquor. Cook diced potatoes and diced onion with just enough hot water to be seen through potatoes. Cook over low heat until done but not mushy. Add clams and bring to a *just below boiling point* for 2 minutes.

Remove from heat and let stand a few minutes, then add scalded milk, clam liquor (strained) and lastly add salt and margarine (or butter).

Personal note: This is a recipe used in my husband's family for many years, his father and grandfather were sea captains. They used clams almost every day whether at sea or at home.

Submitted by Mrs. John E. Stewart, Rockland, Maine

Clam Cakes

2 cups fresh chopped clams
2 eggs, beaten
½ cup clam juice
½ cup cracker crumbs
2 tablespoons flour

1 teaspoon baking powder
1 teaspoon salt
⅛ teaspoon pepper
1 teaspoon sugar

Chop clams after gastric glands have been removed. Drain, reserving the clam water (or juice). Combine eggs and juice.

Prepare crumbs by rolling crackers and measure ½ cup of crumbs into bowl. Mix and sift flour, baking powder, salt, pepper and sugar over the crumbs. Add the egg-clam juice mixture and stir in the clams. Let stand for a few minutes for crumbs to absorb the liquids. If needed, add more juice.

Drop by large spoonfuls into frying pan of hot fat. The fat need not be deep. Cook until golden brown on each side. Serve hot.

Submitted by Mrs. Rita M. Grindle, South Penobscot, Maine

Ed Pert's Devilled Clams

Steam 2 quarts of clams. Remove clams from shells (removing skins from heads) and reserve one cup of clam broth. Reserve the larger clam shells.

Put clams through meat grinder with two hard boiled eggs.

Saute (until golden) 2 large onions well chopped in ½ cup butter.

continued

Add clams and eggs to onions. Then add ½ cup dark bread crumbs and ½ cup light bread crumbs. Mix to pastry consistency. Add enough clam juice to moisten.

Stuff mixture in clam shells. Refrigerate or freeze. When ready to serve, cover each shell with ¼ strip of bacon. To serve, broil until bacon is brown (about 15 minutes).

(Note: Stuffed clams are best when brought to room temperature prior to broiling.) Good luck.

Submitted by Ed Pert, Five Islands, Maine

Clam Batter For Fried Clams

1 egg, beaten
1 cup flour
1½ teaspoons baking powder

⅔ cup sweet milk
½ teaspoon salt

Mix together well. Dip clams in batter, fry in hot deep fat until golden brown. Drain. Very good.

Submitted by Mrs. Crosby E. Prior, Friendship, Maine

Fried Clams

Cracker crumbs
Flour

Milk
Salt, pepper

Mix equal parts cracker crumbs and flour together. Add salt and pepper. Drain or dry clams. Roll clams in the cracker and flour mixture, dip in the milk, then in the crumb mixture again.

Heat vegetable shortening or oil in deep kettle to 375 degrees. Place clams in frying basket and fry until golden brown.

Submitted by Helen Hallowell, Tenants Harbor, Maine

Pan Fried Clams

1 quart raw, shucked clams
2 eggs, beaten
2 cups bread crumbs

½ teaspoon salt
⅛ teaspoon pepper

8

Wash clams, pinch out black part of bellies of large clams.

Dip each clam into dish of beaten eggs, then into dish of bread crumbs to which salt and pepper has been added.

Melt fat in fry pan until ¼" deep. As you fry, keep adding more fat as necessary. Fry until brown.

Submitted by Mrs. Irving H. Parsons, Stockton Springs, Maine

Fried Clams

2 eggs, separated
½ cup milk
1 teaspoon olive oil
1 cup flour

¼ teaspoon salt
1 tablespoon lemon juice
1 pint clams, chopped

Beat yolks of eggs and mix with milk, oil, flour, salt and lemon juice. Beat the whites of eggs stiffly and fold into the above mixture. Fold in the clams last. Set in refrigerator 4 to 5 hours. Drop in hot fat. Serves 5.

Submitted by Nellie Ifemey, Thomaston, Maine

Smothered Clams

Place one quart raw shucked clams in a skillet. Cover with water and simmer till tender. Mix about four tablespoons flour in a little cold water, then add to clams, stirring to make a gravy. Add salt and pepper and other desired seasoning.

(This was a dish my grandmother made.)

Submitted by Priscilla Woodward, Warren, Maine

Clam Casserole

1 pint clams (chopped) and
   juice
1 cup crushed salted crackers
1 cup milk

¼ cup melted margarine
Salt, pepper
1 egg beaten

Mix, turn into casserole, let stand ½ hour. Bake at 350 degrees for 45 minutes.

This is a favorite at our church suppers and all-day work meetings for club.

Submitted by Inga J. Chase, Camden, Maine

Escalloped Clams

1 pint clams with liquor
1 pint cracker crumbs
Butter, salt, pepper

1 egg
1 pint milk

Chop the hard part of the clams and mix with the soft part. Put into a baking dish in alternate layers with the crumbs, crumbs first and last over each layer of clams. Dot with the butter and add salt and pepper. Beat the egg and add to the liquor and milk. Moisten each layer of crumbs thoroughly. Bake in moderate oven 30 minutes or until crumbs are brown on top.

Submitted by Clara W. Thornton, North Haven, Maine

Clam Fritters

1 egg, beaten
2 tablespoons flour
1 teaspoon cream of tartar
½ teaspoon soda

½ teaspoon salt
Clams, cut up (as many as desired)

Sift dry ingredients together, add beaten egg and enough cold water to make soft dough. Mix in the clams and pat into cakes. Fry in hot fat until brown on both sides. Very good.

Submitted by Mrs. Crosby E. Prior, Friendship, Maine

Clam Fritters

1½ cups chopped clams
1½ cups flour
1 teaspoon baking powder

½ teaspoon soda
1 egg, beaten
1 cup sour milk

Mix flour, baking powder and soda together, combine with egg and milk. Add to clams. Fry in well greased frying pan until nicely browned.

Submitted by Leona Starrett, Thomaston, Maine

Clam Fritters

1 pint raw clams
1 egg, beaten
⅓ cup milk

1⅓ cups flour
2 teaspoons baking powder
Salt and pepper

Mix all together and drop in hot fat and fry.

Submitted by Martha Wilson, Thomaston, Maine

Clam Fritters

2 eggs
⅓ cup sweet milk
1⅓ cups sifted flour
½ teaspoon baking soda

1 teaspoon cream of tartar
Salt to taste
1 cup chopped clams (more if
  you like them heavier)

Beat eggs and milk together, stir in flour sifted together with soda, cream of tartar and salt. Add the chopped clams all at once and mix until clams are coated. Fry in deep fat or in a frying pan with about ½ inch of fat. These should be made with fresh Maine clams only.

Submitted by Irma W. Benner, South Harpswell, Maine

Clam Fritters

2 eggs
⅓ cup milk
1⅓ cups flour, sifted
2 teaspoons cream of tartar
1 teaspoon soda

Salt and pepper
1½ pints chopped clams (just
  as good with 2 cans of
  minced clams)

Beat eggs until well blended, add milk, flour sifted with cream of tartar and soda, seasoned with salt and pepper. Mix in clams. Fry in hot fat till golden brown.

Submitted by Mrs. Eugene Doran, Rockland, Maine

Clam Fritters

Take 50 small or 25 large sand clams from their shells; if large, cut each in two. Lay them on a thickly folded napkin; put a pint bowl of wheat flour into a basin, add to it two well-beaten eggs, half a pint of sweet milk, and nearly as much of their own liquor. Beat the batter until it is smooth and perfectly free from lumps; then stir in the clams. Put plenty of lard or beef fat into a thick-bottomed frying pan, let it become boiling hot; put in the batter by the spoonful; let them fry gently. When one side is a delicate brown, turn the other.

Submitted by L. G. Tennies, Westport Island, Wiscasset, Maine

CLAM PUFFS are good at any meal. (Recipe on Page 13)

Clam Puffs

These used to be very popular when we served dinners here many years ago and have been immensely popular at the Maine Seafoods Festival in Rockland ever since they have been served there.

Maine Seafoods Festival specialty batter may be thinned and used for fried onion rings, too.

If canned clams are used, the liquor can be used to thin out the batter. Fresh Maine clams are larger than littlenecks; after squeezing out the black area from the clams, you'll need to cut them up into small pieces with shears.

1 tablespoon melted butter
1 egg, beaten
1 cup milk
1 pint fresh clams, chopped

(1½ cups flour sifted together with 1 level tablespoon plus 1 teaspoon baking powder, and ½ teaspoon salt)

Add the beaten egg to the melted butter and milk. Sift baking powder, flour and salt mixture. Add the chopped clams drained of liquor and mix with the batter. Make in balls the size of a walnut (a soupspoon will make one large or two small puffs). Deep fat fry at 375 degrees, NO HIGHER. When brown they are cooked.

Submitted by Cap'n Ote Lewis, Ash Point, Maine

Mother's Clam Pats

1 pint chopped clams
2 eggs, beaten
⅓ cup flour

2 teaspoons baking powder
¼ teaspoon salt
Shake a little pepper

Combine eggs, flour, baking powder, salt and pepper, mix in clams.

Put skillet on medium heat, add 2½ tablespoons bacon drippings or shortening. Drop batter from large spoon and fry until brown on both sides.

Best way is to cook slowly. Serve with tartar sauce. You may substitute 2 cans minced clams, drained, when fresh clams are not available.

Submitted by Gwen Church Ellis, Warren, Maine

Fricassee Of Hen Clams

Hen clams are a special variety of clams, found in certain spots in this area at especially low tides, and found elsewhere also, I presume. They appear similar to "skimmers" which are dragged up in deeper waters off Long Island, N. Y.

These clams are relatively huge, measuring easily 4" to 6" across. I steam them open the same way as cooking regular steamed clams. I remove and clean the meats and put them through a meat grinder. With the resulting chopped clam meat I make the following which is delicious. The hen clam has a slightly stronger flavor and the addition of sherry to this recipe somewhat curtails the strong flavor and makes it a special treat.

Put in a saucepan

2 tablespoons butter
1 pint chopped clams
2 tablespoons flour
   Stir in gradually
½ cup cream
   Stir and cook 1 minute.

Salt and cayenne to taste
   Stir in
1 egg yolk, slightly beaten
Season to taste with cooking
   sherry (at least ¼ cup)
Serve on toast or in patty shells

Submitted by Mrs. Donald Stewart, Castine, Maine

Quahog Cakes

1 cup flour
2 cups quahogs, ground fine
¼ cup milk
2 eggs

3 teaspoons baking powder
½ teaspoon salt
Dash pepper

Beat the eggs and add milk. Sift flour with baking powder, salt and pepper. Add flour to the egg mixture. Stir in the quahogs. Drop by spoonfuls into a frying pan which contains a small amount of vegetable oil. Cook on both sides until a golden brown.

Submitted by Mrs. Arthur S. Wyllie, Warren, Maine

Quahog Casserole

2 cups milk
2 cups cracker crumbs
2 cups quahogs, ground fine
4 eggs

1 teaspoon salt
¼ teaspoon pepper
Butter

Mix milk and crackers and let stand for a few minutes. Add clams (quahogs), eggs, salt and pepper. Pour into a 2-quart baking dish and dot with butter. Bake in a 350 degree oven for about 1 hour, or until done. Test with a knife.

Submitted by Mrs. Arthur S. Wyllie, Warren, Maine

Baked Stuffed Hen Clams

1 peck hen clams (or you may use quahogs)
2 rolls round salted crackers, crushed

¼ pound butter, melted
2 tablespoons Worcestershire sauce
2 tablespoons cooking sherry

Shuck clams, being very careful not to crack the larger shells that will be used to bake the stuffing. Keep hinges intact. Allow one or two 4"-5" shells per person. Scrub shells well that are to be used.

Pinch out bellies (black part) of shucked clams and remove black strip. Put through coarse blade of grinder. Put in colander to drain, but reserve juice to moisten stuffing, if necessary.

Meanwhile, crush 1 or 2 rolls of crackers, depending on the amount of ground clams used. Add half the amount of melted butter to crackers, also Worcestershire sauce and sherry.

Stuff lower half of shell until rounded full. Drizzle remaining butter over each lower half. Close cover and wire shut with "mechanics" wire in V shape.

Bake on pan at 350 degrees for 45 minutes.

(Minced canned clams may be substituted and baked in individual serving dishes.)

Submitted by Mrs. Irving H. Parsons, Stockton Springs, Maine

CRABMEAT UNIQUE has a bonus — Maine's famed potatoes.
Tuna may also be used for filling. (Recipe on Page 23)

Crabmeat Delight

½ cup melted butter
½ teaspoon salt
Dash pepper
1 teaspoon dry mustard
2 teaspoons Worcestershire
sauce

½ cup flour
3 cups milk
2 beaten egg yolks
2 cups crabmeat
Buttered bread crumbs

Melt butter in saucepan, add the seasonings with Worcestershire sauce. Add flour and let bubble until thoroughly combined. Gradually add milk, stir in beaten egg yolks and crabmeat. Pour into a 1½-quart casserole, top with buttered crumbs. Bake at 400 degrees for 20 minutes.

Submitted by Mrs. Robert Sowton, Jr., Camden, Maine

Crab Delight

2 tablespoons chopped peppers
2 tablespoons butter
2 tablespoons flour
½ teaspoon mustard
¼ teaspoon salt
¼ teaspoon Worcestershire
sauce

Dash cayenne
1 cup grated cheese
1 cup tomatoes (strained)
¾ cup milk
1 egg beaten
1 cup or more crabmeat

Saute pepper in butter for 5 minutes. Add flour, seasonings, cheese, tomatoes and egg. Heat the milk and add to the first mixture, and lastly, add crabmeat. Serve on toast rounds or in patty shells.

Submitted by Lulu M. Miller, Waldoboro, Maine

Crab Louis

1 cup mayonnaise
½ cup cream
4 tablespoons chili sauce
1 teaspoon minced parsley

1 green pepper, chopped
3 stuffed olives, chopped
1 cup crabmeat (or more)

Mix together well and serve on leaves of lettuce.

Submitted by Mrs. Leland Foster, Wiscasset, Maine

Crabmeat Casserole

1 cup bread crumbs
1 pound crabmeat
3 eggs, beaten
3 cups milk

½ cup grated cheese
2 tablespoons grated onion
Salt and pepper
Butter

In a baking dish make a layer of ⅓ cup bread crumbs, ¼ cup cheese, half of the crabmeat and 1 tablespoon onion. Repeat with a second layer. Bring the milk to a boil and add slowly to the beaten eggs. Add salt and pepper to casserole and pour milk-egg mixture over layers. Top with remaining crumbs, dot with butter and bake at 350 degrees for 40 minutes.

Submitted by Bodine Ames, Vinalhaven, Maine

Crab Casserole

1 can frozen shrimp soup
(defrosted)
⅔ cup milk
¼ pound grated sharp cheese
½ cup mayonnaise

2 cups of very fine noodles,
uncooked
1 cup or ½ pound Maine
crabmeat
1 (3 oz.) can onion rings

Mix shrimp soup with milk, mayonnaise, noodles and crabmeat. Pour into a greased baking dish and sprinkle the grated cheese over top. Cover tightly and bake for 20 minutes at 350 degrees. Add onion rings and bake uncovered for another 10 to 15 minutes. An excellent luncheon for 4.

Submitted by Mrs. Edward F. Dow, Orono, Maine

Crab Casserole

1½ cups mayonnaise
1 cup soft bread crumbs
1 cup cream or evaporated milk
6 hard-cooked eggs
1 cup crabmeat

1 tablespoon chopped
parsley

3 slices buttered bread,
cubed

Thoroughly mix all ingredients except bread cubes. Turn into casserole and top with bread cubes. Bake at 300 degrees for 45 to 50 minutes.

Submitted by Margaret Jenny, Belgrade, Maine

Crabmeat Casserole

1 green pepper, chopped
2 pimentos, diced
1 teaspoon prepared mustard
Salt-pepper

2 eggs, beaten
1 cup mayonnaise
1 pound crabmeat
Paprika

Mix together the green pepper, pimentos, mustard, salt, pepper, beaten eggs, and mayonnaise. Gently fold in the crabmeat. Spoon into a buttered casserole. Spread lightly with a coating of mayonnaise and sprinkle with paprika. Bake 350 degrees for 25 minutes. Serve hot.

Submitted by Ruth A. Savage, Palmyra, Maine

Crabmeat Casserole

8 oz. cooked spaghetti
1 can mushroom soup
¼ cup diced onion
2 cups grated cheese
1½ cups crabmeat

1 cup milk
1 tablespoon pimento
2 hard-cooked eggs
Chopped olives
2 tablespoons melted butter

Combine spaghetti with soup, onion, cheese, crabmeat and milk. Pour into a buttered baking dish. Top with the pimento, eggs, olives and melted butter. Bake at 400 degrees for 30 minutes. This is a favorite recipe at social gatherings on Deer Isle.

Submitted by Priscilla Woodward, Warren, Maine

Crabmeat Casserole

½ cup margarine
⅔ cup flour
2⅔ cups milk
1 cup sharp cheese, shredded
8 ounce package frozen or
   fresh crabmeat
2 cups celery, sliced
½ green pepper, chopped

2 pimentos, chopped
⅓ cup blanched almonds,
   chopped or sliced
4 hard cooked eggs, sliced
2 teaspoons salt
Pepper to taste
Sherry to taste
Buttered crumbs

Melt margarine, blend in flour, add milk to make cream sauce. Add cheese, cook at low heat until cheese is melted. Add other ingredients, sprinkle top with buttered crumbs. Bake at 350 degrees for 45 minutes. Serves 8-10.

Submitted by Elizabeth H. Cutliffe, North Edgecomb, Maine

Crabmeat-Macaroni Casserole

1 pound fresh crabmeat or 2 cans (7½ oz. each), drained
¼ cup butter or margarine
¼ cup flour
2 teaspoons salt
⅛ teaspoon pepper
1 teaspoon minced onion (instant)
3¼ cups milk
1½ cups uncooked macaroni (elbow or small shells)
1 can (6 oz.) sliced mushrooms, drained
½ cup grated sharp Cheddar cheese

Flake crabmeat with a fork, removing bones. Cook macaroni according to directions on the package and when done, drain well.

While macaroni is cooking, melt butter in a saucepan. Remove from heat and stir in flour, salt and pepper to make a smooth paste. Add milk gradually, stirring to blend well. Add onion. Over medium heat bring to a boil, stirring all the time. When it boils, reduce heat and simmer for 5 minutes.

Combine macaroni with crabmeat, mushrooms and sauce. Mix well. Pour into a 2-quart casserole. Sprinkle the top with cheese.

Bake at 350 degrees for 20 minutes or until cheese is melted and it is bubbly. Makes 6 to 8 generous servings.

Submitted by Margaret F. Stevens, Glen Cove, Maine

Crab And Shrimp Casserole

1 cup cleaned, cooked shrimp
1 cup diced celery
¼ cup shopped green pepper
2 tablespoons finely chopped onion
1 can (7½ oz.) crabmeat
½ teaspoon salt
1 teaspoon Worcestershire sauce
¾ cup mayonnaise
Bread crumbs

Mix all ingredients together and put into a 1-quart casserole. Cover with bread crumbs and bake at 350 degrees for 30 to 35 minutes. Serves 4.

Submitted by Mrs. Alexander C. Stewart, Waldoboro, Maine

Crab Biscuits

1 pound crabmeat	1 cup of sifted flour with
2 tablespoons mayonnaise	1½ teaspoons baking powder
1 egg	Flour to coat
1 tablespoon grated onion	Milk to moisten
8 pieces of bread OR	Fat to fry
1 cup dry biscuit mix OR	

Mix together the egg, onion and mayonnaise. Soak the bread or flour mixture in the milk (should not be too moist) and add to the egg mixture. Add the crabmeat. Chill for 1 hour. Make into balls about the size of an egg. Roll in flour and fry in deep fat at 350 degrees. Serve with melted butter.

Submitted by Bodine Ames, Vinalhaven, Maine

A Good Weight Watcher Lunch

1 slice of bread	1 oz. grated cheese
3 oz. crabmeat	Milk
1 tablespoon mayonnaise	

Mix mayonnaise with a little milk to make it smooth. Add to the crabmeat and spread on the bread. Shake the cheese over it and broil until a light brown.

Submitted by Bodine Ames, Vinalhaven, Maine

Crabmeat Scallop

1 can mushroom soup	¼ teaspoon pepper
1 tablespoon flour	1 pound crabmeat
1 tablespoon margarine	1½ cups soft bread crumbs
⅜ pound mild cheese	2 tablespoons butter, melted
½ teaspoon salt	

Thicken soup with flour and margarine. Melt cheese, add salt and pepper. Add to the soup mixture, add crabmeat. Put in buttered casserole, cover with bread crumbs and drizzle butter over top. Bake in a 350 degree oven for 30 minutes.

Submitted by Mrs. Austin W. Miller, Friendship, Maine

Crabmeat Mornay

4 tablespoons butter
2½ tablespoons cornstarch
3 tablespoons flour
¾ teaspoon salt
¾ cup chicken stock

¾ cup milk
2 egg yolks
1½ cups crabmeat
½ cup grated cheese

Melt butter, add cornstarch, flour and salt. Stir until well-blended. Pour stock on gradually, while stirring constantly. Bring to boiling point and boil for 3 minutes. Add milk gradually, stirring constantly. Bring to boiling point again and add egg yolks bit by bit.

Butter ramekin dishes. Cover bottoms with crabmeat, pour on sauce, sprinkle with cheese. Cook in broiling oven to melt cheese and brown. (A most delicious dish if you can spend the time doing it.)

Submitted by Josephine C. Philbrick, Camden, Maine

Quick Crab a la Creole

1 package fresh crabmeat or
  1 can crabmeat
1 can cream of tomato soup
⅓ can of milk

1 tablespoon prepared mustard
1 tablespoon hot ketchup
6 slices toast

Mix all ingredients together and heat. Serve hot on slices of toast

Submitted by Mrs. Carl Otto, Orono, Maine

Crab With Mushrooms

4 tablespoons butter
1 tablespoon minced onion
1 cup sliced mushrooms
3 tablespoons flour
½ teaspoon salt

½ teaspoon mustard
Nutmeg, pepper
½ cup milk
2 cups flaked crabmeat

Melt butter, add onion and mushrooms. Cook 3 minutes. Stir in flour and seasonings. Add milk gradually and stir over a low fire until sauce is smooth and thick. Add crabmeat, heat and serve on toast points or in patty shells.

Submitted by Josephine C. Philbrick, Camden, Maine

Crabmeat Salad
Maine crabmeat goes Polynesian

½ pound crabmeat (cooked and cleaned)

1 can (20 oz.) pineapple chunks, drained

2 large avocados, peeled and sliced

1 medium head lettuce, crisp, bite-size pieces

Toss all into a wooden salad bowl and serve with an extra bowl of sour cream. More crabmeat may be added to this salad and used as a main dish. This is really a new approach to crabmeat salad. It is tasty, attractive and delicious.

Submitted by Helen Wooster, Waldoboro, Maine

Seafood Sauce
For Maine Crabmeat and Other Seafood

1 cup mayonnaise

1 cup chili sauce

¼ cup sweet pickle relish

1½ teaspoons prepared mustard

1 tablespoon chopped chives (can use ½ teaspoon onion)

2 cups chopped hard-cooked eggs

1 cup finely chopped celery

1 teaspoon grated lemon rind

2 tablespoons lemon juice

Salt and pepper to taste

Combine all of the ingredients and blend well. Serve with Maine crabmeat, shrimp or other seafood on lettuce or in a salad.

Submitted by Mrs. Eldred Hough, Orono, Maine

Crabmeat Unique

1 cup crabmeat

1 tablespoon grated onion

2 tablespoons butter

4 tablespoons milk

¼ teaspoon red pepper

6 medium-sized potatoes

½ teaspoon salt

½ cup grated cheese

Bake potatoes, cut them lengthwise and scrape out. Add butter, milk, onion and seasoning. Mix well. Now add the crabmeat and refill the potato shells. Sprinkle with grated cheese on top of each. Place in oven until cheese melts.

Submitted by Grace Irvine, Warren, Maine

Crabmeat Salad Sandwich Filling

1 pound Maine crabmeat
2 tablespoons fresh lemon juice
Few drops of onion juice
Salt, pepper

Mayonnaise
Bread
Butter or margarine
Chopped celery (optional)

Pick over crabmeat to remove any bit of shell. Add lemon juice and refrigerate overnight. When ready to make the sandwiches, cream butter or margarine and spread the bread lightly on both slices. To the crabmeat add a few drops of onion juice (cut an onion crosswise and scrape juice from cut surface), add mayonnaise with salt and pepper to taste. If you wish to make the filling go farther, add the chopped celery, about ½ cup. Spread the filling on the buttered bread and top with the other buttered slice. Wrap in wax paper and refrigerate. Trim and cut at serving time. This filling may be used to fill tiny cream puff shells.

Submitted by Mrs. Francis Raynes, York, Maine

Crab And Rice Squares With Shrimp Sauce

¼ cup minced onion
¼ cup minced parsley
¼ cup diced pimento
1 teaspoon salt
1 cup grated American
cheese
1 teaspoon Worcestershire
sauce

½ pound fresh crabmeat (can
use frozen or canned)
3 eggs, slightly beaten
2 cups milk
3 cups cooked rice

Mix together onion, parsley, pimento, salt, cheese and Worcestershire sauce. Add to the crabmeat. Add the beaten eggs with the milk and rice. Pour into a greased baking dish (I use rectangular ovenproof glass type). Bake at 325 degrees for 45 minutes. Cut in squares and serve with sauce.

Shrimp Sauce

1 can frozen shrimp soup
½ cup sour cream
1 teaspoon lemon juice
¼ teaspoon curry powder.

Thaw the frozen soup, add cream, lemon juice and curry powder. Heat carefully and serve over squares.

Submitted by Jean L. Dotton, Dover, New Hampshire

Lobster Chowder

4-5 pounds lobsters
4 crackers (pounded)
1 quart boiling milk

Butter, ½ size of egg
Pepper and salt.

Cook lobsters, take out meat and chop fine. Take the green part and add to the pounded crackers, stir this into the boiling milk. Then add the lobster, butter, pepper and salt and bring to a boil.

Taken from an old cookbook in the late 1800's.

Submitted by Ada M. Spencer, Bradley, Maine

Dakin's Lobster Stew

1 pound lobster meat
1 teaspoon chopped onion
1 quart milk

1 cup instant mashed potatoes
Salt, pepper, butter
¼ cup dark sherry

1. Saute lobster meat with onion, lightly, using small pat of butter in top of double boiler.
2. Add 1 quart milk, stir in the mashed potato, stir softly, heat through.
3. Add butter, salt, very little pepper to taste, and
4. Let it set for 6-8 hours.
5. Upon heating to serve, add sherry and float another pat of butter. Suggest double boiler be used both in preparing and in reheating.
6. Serve piping hot.

P. S. This recipe comes from the lobster stew suppers my dad, Ernest A. Dakin, helped serve at the Masons Meetings, New Sharon, Maine.

Submitted by June Rose, New Sharon, Maine

Lobster Stew

1 pound lobster meat, diced
Butter size of egg
3 crackers

Salt and pepper
1 quart milk
Tomalley

Fry the lobster meat in the butter for a few minutes (this makes the stew red). Roll the crackers fine and rub into the tomalley, add a little salt and pepper. Add to the lobster meat. Heat the milk and pour slowly on this paste and the lobster. Let come to a boil and serve.

Submitted by Mrs. Edward Kiskila, Friendship, Maine

Doris' Lobster Stew

3 cups cooked lobster meat,
  cut up (about 3 1½-pound
  lobsters)
6 tablespoons butter

7 cups milk
1 teaspoon salt
⅛ teaspoon pepper
Tomalley from lobster

Remove the meat from the cooked lobsters, cut up. Saute slowly in the butter (no substitute) over low heat. Set aside to cool. Heat the milk to scalding. Slowly add the lobster meat and tomalley with the salt and pepper. Stir to blend. Set off the heat for 2 hours; reheat to serve.

(Plan to make this stew 3 hours before serving time for blending.)

Submitted by Mrs. Carl Dow, Winthrop, Maine

Deviled Lobster

5 pounds lobster in shell
1 pint of cream
2 level tablespoons flour
2 heaping tablespoons butter

⅔ tablespoon dry mustard
½ teaspoon cayenne
Buttered crumbs

Cook the lobster and cut meat into small pieces. Set aside.

Heat the cream, mix dry ingredients with butter and add to the cream. Cook until smooth. Put in the lobster pieces.

Place in casserole and cover with buttered crumbs. Bake in hot oven until it bubbles. Delicious. Will serve 10 persons.

Submitted by Elizabeth Shyne, Rockland, Maine

Baked Stuffed Lobster

Lobsters (1 each serving)
2 cups salted cracker crumbs
  per lobster

¼ cup butter per lobster

Boil lobsters — put on back and cut from head to tail about ½ inch deep. Take out brain and black strip from tail. Crack the claws and butter the cracks. Remove tomalley from cavity. Mix together the cracker crumbs, tomalley, butter and ¼ cup hot water to make a stuffing. Stuff the lobster and bake at 400 degrees until stuffing is golden brown, about 20 minutes. Bake on a cookie sheet. Serve hot.

Submitted by Gertrude Hupper, Tenants Harbor, Maine

Baked Stuffed Lobster

1 lobster for each person, 1¼ to 1½ pounds each. The amounts listed below are for one lobster.

Sauce

¾ tablespoon butter
¾ tablespoon flour
½ cup light stock (may be chicken or made with bouillon cube)

¼ teaspoon dry mustard
1 teaspoon minced onion (instant)
Salt and pepper to taste

For Lobster Mixture

2 tablespoons butter or margarine

1 tablespoon cream
2 egg yolks

For Crumbs

⅓ cup butter or margarine
1 cup bread crumbs

Parmesan cheese and sherry if desired

Split the lobster in half (head to tail), crack claws. Also remove "other matter" from shell and discard. Remove meat and chop. To make the sauce, melt butter in a saucepan, stir in flour until blended, then slowly add the stock while stirring. Add mustard, onion, salt and pepper. Blend well. Leave on low heat.

To make lobster mixture: melt butter in another saucepan. Saute lobster meat until it is hot and begins to turn pink. Add the boiling sauce and simmer together for 2 minutes. Beat together the cream and egg yolks and pour a little of the hot mixture into the cream-egg. Add to the lobster mixture.

For buttered crumbs, melt ⅓ cup of butter in saucepan and add bread crumbs. Mix well so bread is well covered with fat.

Fill lobster shells with lobster mixture, and cover with crumbs. You may sprinkle with Parmesan cheese (over the crumbs). Bake or broil in a 375 degree oven until crumbs are a light golden brown. If desired, 2 tablespoons sherry may be poured over all before serving.

Submitted by Margaret F. Stevens, Glen Cove, Maine

Down-East Lobster Newburg

2 cups milk	1 tablespoon lemon juice
¼ cup butter	Dash cayenne pepper
¼ cup flour	4 egg yolks, beaten
2 cups lobster meat	½ cup sherry wine

Make a white sauce with the milk, butter and flour, in double boiler over hot water. Add lobster meat sauteed in butter, add lemon juice, pepper and egg yolks. Season with the wine. Serve on toast tips. 4 servings.

Submitted by Georgia Kennett, Canton, Maine

Lobster Newburg

2 cups boiled, diced lobster meat	2 egg yolks, beaten
4 tablespoons melted butter	¼ teaspoon salt
1 tablespoon flour	1 teaspoon lemon juice
1 cup cream or milk	Paprika

Heat lobster in 3 tablespoons melted butter, do not let burn. In another saucepan stir flour into other tablespoon butter, then add cream, heat, stir until smooth. When boiling starts, remove from fire, add beaten egg yolks and stir until mixture thickens. Add diced lobster and seasonings. Do not heat again or mixture may curdle.

Serve on crackers or thin toast.

Submitted by Martha Wilson, Thomaston, Maine

Lobster Newberg

3 cups cooked lobster	Butter
1 cup light cream	Seasonings
2 egg yolks, beaten	

Heat cream and egg yolks in double boiler, cook until it thickens. Add the lobster, cut fine, cook 10 minutes. Add butter and season to taste. A little brandy adds to the flavor also. Serve on crisp crackers or toasted bread. 4-5 servings. Scallops or crabmeat can also be used with this recipe.

Submitted by Orilla Sampson, North Haven, Maine

Lobster Newberg

1 (2-pound) lobster, cooked
2 heaping tablespoons butter
½ teaspoon salt

2 tablespoons sherry
2 egg yolks, beaten
1 cup cream

Cut meat from the lobster into small pieces. Combine lobster with the butter and heat. Add salt, sherry, beaten egg yolks and cream. Cook and stir until thickened.

Submitted by Emily Merrill, Newport, Maine

Lobster Casserole

¾ to 1 pound lobster meat
3 tablespoons butter
3 tablespoons flour
¾ teaspoon dry mustard
Salt and pepper

1 cup heavy cream or
  evaporated milk
½ cup rich milk
2 or 3 slices bread
  (remove crusts)

Cut lobster into bite-size pieces and cook slowly in butter for color, do not overcook or cook too fast or lobster will be tough. Remove lobster meat, add flour mixed with seasonings to fat in pan. Add cream and milk slowly. Cook, stirring constantly until thick. Add lobster meat and bread crumbs torn in small pieces. Pour into greased casserole. Top with a few buttered crumbs. Bake until bubbly and lightly browned. If desired, you can add sherry before baking.

Submitted by Mrs. Austin W. Miller, Friendship, Maine

Lobster Rice Casserole

½ cup rice
1½ cups water
1 can frozen shrimp soup
1 soup can milk
1 cup fresh or frozen lobster meat
8 oz. can sliced mushrooms

1 cup ripe olives, sliced
¼ cup chopped green pepper
Salt, pepper and herbs to taste
  (thyme or oregano)

Cook rice in water until done. Thaw soup in milk. Add cooked rice and all other ingredients. Place in casserole. Bake 50-60 minutes at 350 degrees. Serves 6.

Submitted by Elizabeth H. Cutliffe, North Edgecomb, Maine

Lobster Casserole

2 tablespoons butter
2 tablespoons flour
½ teaspoon dry mustard
Salt, pepper
1 cup thinned canned cream

2½ cups canned milk
1 pound lobster meat
5 slices bread
Buttered crumbs

Make cream sauce as follows: Melt the butter, add flour, dry mustard, salt and pepper. Slowly add the cream and milk. Stir until smooth and thick. Add lobster meat and the bread cut into cubes. Put into casserole, top with buttered bread crumbs. Bake at 350 degrees until crumbs are brown.

Submitted by Goldie Chadwick, Thomaston, Maine

Sunday Night Lobster Delight

4 tablespoons butter
5 tablespoons flour
2 cups milk
1 teaspoon salt
½ teaspoon dry mustard

⅛ teaspoon white pepper
½ cup strong Cheddar cheese
1 cup fresh cooked lobster, minced
¼ cup of juice from lobster

Melt butter in saucepan, add flour and mix well. Add cold milk, slowly stirring until smooth and creamy. Add salt, dry mustard and pepper which has been mixed together and boil about 3 minutes. Add the cheese cut into bits and stir until blended. Lastly, add the lobster and juice. Serve on toast points, sprinkle with paprika. Serves 4. Crabmeat, tuna or shrimp may be used.

Submitted by Beatrice M. Chase, Waldoboro, Maine

Lobster Omelet

4 eggs
4 tablespoons milk
Salt and pepper to taste
Approx. 2 tablespoons butter
or margarine

½ cup lobster meat (which has
been cut into small pieces
and warmed in butter)

Beat eggs until light and fluffy. Add milk, salt and pepper. Heat butter in omelet pan. Add egg mixture and cook slowly over low heat. When underside is set, lift omelet slightly with spatula to let uncooked portion flow underneath and cook. When mixture is almost set, spread warmed lobster meat on top, fold omelet, and cook an additional couple of minutes. Serves 2.

Submitted by Eleanor C. Linton, Camden, Maine

Mussel Chowder

2 tablespoons butter
4 medium potatoes, diced
(about 2 cups)
1 medium onion, chopped
About 1½ cups shucked
mussels (cooked in ¼ cup
sherry just to open; save
broth)

2 cups mussel broth,
strained
3 cups whole milk plus 1 cup
light cream

Saute the chopped onion in butter till golden. Add potatoes
and mussel broth barely to cover. Simmer over low heat until
done (about 15 minutes). Add the mussels and cook for 2 minutes
after it comes to a full boil. Meanwhile, scald the milk and cream.
Remove the chowder pot from heat and let stand for 5 minutes
before adding the scalded milk and rest of mussel broth. More
sherry may be added if desired. Season to taste with salt and
pepper. Before serving, add 1 tablespoon butter. If possible, make
a day or two before serving and let marinate in refrigerator. Serves
6-8.

Submitted by Mrs. Bartram Cadbury, Cushing, Maine

Dry Mussel Stew

Take 12 large mussels (shucked) and cook in half a pint of
their own liquor. Season with butter and white pepper. Cook for
5 minutes, stirring constantly. Serve in hot soup plates or bowls.
Hot cream can be added but is apt to curdle.

Submitted by Gertrude Hupper, Tenants Harbor, Maine

Scalloped Mussels

Clean the mussels well, put 2 in each half shell. To each shell add a dash of white pepper, half a teaspoon minced celery. Dice 2 slices of bacon and spread ½ teaspoon on each shell. Dust with cracker crumbs. Put a small piece of butter on top and bake until brown.

Submitted by Gertrude L. Hupper, Tenants Harbor, Maine

Deviled Mussels

1 quart shucked mussels with their juice
2 tablespoons salad oil
¼ cup minced onion
1 cup cracker crumbs
2 tablespoons Worcestershire sauce
2 tablespoons catsup
4 dashes Tabasco
Juice of ½ lemon
2 tablespoons minced parsley
1 tablespoon butter

Heat mussels in their juice. Heat the oil and saute the onion lightly. Stir in crumbs, Worcestershire, catsup, Tabasco, lemon juice and parsley. Stir mussels and their juice into the crumb mixture and turn into a shallow casserole. Top with bits of butter and bake 15 minutes in a 425 degree oven until sizzling. Serves 4 or 5. Serve with a green salad.

Submitted by Gertrude L. Hupper, Tenants Harbor, Maine

Baked Mussels

60 Maine mussels
Salt, pepper
1 teaspoon minced onion
Sliced bacon
Parmesan cheese

Scrub and wash mussels and steam as for steamed clams. Remove from shells, trim off beard with scissors and place in buttered baking dish. Season with salt, pepper and onion. Cover with thin slices of bacon and sprinkle with cheese. Bake in moderate oven, 350 degrees, for 15 minutes.

Submitted by Mrs. Goldie Chadwick, Thomaston, Maine

Fried Mussels

Freshly shucked mussels
2 tablespoons butter and lard
  mixed

Salt and pepper
Beaten egg
Fine cracker crumbs

Take freshly shucked mussels from their own liquor and dry on folded paper towel or napkin. Heat butter and lard in a thick-bottomed frying pan. Season the mussels with salt and pepper, then dip in beaten egg, then fine cracker crumbs. Fry in the hot fat until a delicate brown, turning with a broad-bladed knife under them. Serve crisp and hot.

Submitted by Gertrude L. Hupper, Tenants Harbor, Maine

Fried Mussels

To prepare mussels in shells: First clean and wash. Put as much water as will cover them in a kettle, add salt and when boiling put in the mussels. In about 5 minutes the shells will open. Drain and take out of shells, beard them also clean from stones, moss and gravel. Wash in warm water, wipe dry. Flour and fry in butter until crisp. Serve with melted butter, juice of orange and snipped parsley.

Submitted by Gertrude L. Hupper, Tenants Harbor, Maine

Roast Mussels In Shell

Roast in an iron fry pan or in shallow pan in hot oven. When they open, empty the juice into a saucepan and add the shucked mussels. For each 6 mussels, add a tablespoon butter with a dash of salt and pepper.

Submitted by Gertrude L. Hupper, Tenants Harbor, Maine

Little Pigs In Blankets Or Oyster Bundles

24 large oysters
24 very thin slices of bacon
Salt and pepper

Parsley
Slices of toast

Season oysters with salt and pepper, then wrap each oyster in one slice of bacon and fasten with a toothpick. Heat a frying pan and put in the oysters. Cook on one side and then the other, just long enough to crisp the bacon, about 5 minutes. Cut slices of toast into quarters and place an oyster on each small piece of toast. Garnish with parsley. Serve immediately.

Submitted by Lulu M. Miller, Waldoboro, Maine

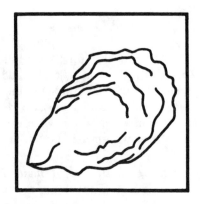

Holiday Scalloped Oysters

1 pint oysters
16 common crackers (unsalted)
⅓ to ½ cup butter

Salt and pepper to taste
2¾ cups whole milk

Butter well a 2-quart casserole. Over bottom crush 4 crackers rather coarsely. Over this place ⅓ of the oysters, dot part of the butter over oysters and sprinkle with salt and pepper. Repeat this layer twice, topping with remaining 4 crackers and butter left. Pour milk carefully over all and let stand several hours to absorb as much milk as possible. Turn top layer under once before baking. Bake at 350 degrees for 45 minutes.

Submitted by Mrs. Austin W. Miller, Friendship, Maine
and Elizabeth Shyne, Rockland, Maine

Scalloped Oysters

1 pint oysters
2½ packages crushed salted crackers (from a 1-pound box)

1 stick oleo or butter
Salt and pepper
2 cups milk (more if needed)

Butter a casserole and sprinkle with a layer of cracker crumbs, then a layer of oysters. Add a little salt and pepper and thin slices of oleo. Alternate layers, ending with cracker crumbs. Add milk until ingredients are moist. Bake in a 325 degree oven 40 to 55 minutes.

Submitted by Mrs. William D. Murphy, Jr., Elliot, Maine

Scalloped Oysters

1 pint oysters
½ cup bread crumbs
½ cup cracker crumbs
½ cup melted butter

Salt and pepper
4 tablespoons oyster liquor
2 tablespoons milk or cream

Mix bread and cracker crumbs, stir in butter. Put a thin layer of crumbs in baking dish, cover with oysters, sprinkle with salt and pepper, add ½ of oyster liquor and cream. Repeat. Cover top with remaining crumbs. Bake 30 minutes in 375 degree oven.

Submitted by Martha Wilson, Thomaston, Maine

Oyster Casserole

½ pint oysters
1½ cups macaroni elbows
⅓ cup butter or oleo

⅓ cup flour
1½ cups milk
Cracker crumbs

Cook oysters in their own juice until edges curl — as for a stew. Cook macaroni elbows as directed, and drain. Make a medium white sauce by melting the butter over low heat, stir in flour and add milk. Stir until thickens. Layer oysters and macaroni in a baking dish, cover with the white sauce, sprinkle with cracker crumbs and bake at 350 degrees for 30 minutes.

Submitted by Florence Parsons, Newport, Maine

Oysters Fried In Batter

Oysters
2 eggs
1 small cup milk

Flour to make a batter
Salt, pepper
Lard or butter for frying

Drain oysters and dip each in batter made with eggs, milk, flour, salt and pepper to taste. Fry in a small amount of butter or lard. Turn with a broad-bladed knife. Serve hot. (Some of the oyster liquid can be added to the batter if preferred.)

Submitted by Josephine C. Philbrick, Camden, Maine

Oyster Fromage

1 pint oysters
½ pound cheese

2 slices of bread buttered generously

Place bread in a well-buttered casserole and place half of the oysters on top. Season well with salt, pepper and cayenne. Cover with half of the cheese and repeat layer. Cover with bread crumbs and make a sauce as follows:

2 eggs
1½ cups milk

1 teaspoon mustard
Paprika

Mix well and pour over the oyster mixture in the casserole. Bake at 350 degrees about 30 minutes.

Submitted by Charlotte C. Hopkins, Rockland, Maine

Pickled 'Wrinkles'

Large sea periwinkles
1 cup of wine vinegar

¼ cup of sugar
1 tablespoon whole allspice

Steam the periwinkles in 1 inch of water, slightly salted, for 20 minutes. (Use the periwinkles with the ridged shells, not the smooth kind. We call them 'wrinkles' here on the island.) Dig out of the shell, cut off stomach end and flat piece on top. Cover the meat in a jar with the vinegar, sugar and whole allspice. Shake hard and let set a couple of hours in the refrigerator, but serve at room temperature to bring out the flavor. (Will keep indefinitely in the refrigerator, but you might want to remove the allspice after a couple of days as the flavor will get very strong.)

Submitted by Bodine Ames, Vinalhaven, Maine

Marinated Scallops

1 quart fresh scallops
1 cup salad oil
¼ cup white tarragon wine
    vinegar
¼ cup lemon juice

1 clove garlic, pressed
1 teaspoon parsley
1 teaspoon sweet basil
½ teaspoon oregano
2 teaspoons powdered sugar

Drain scallops, small scallops leave whole, large ones cut in bite-size pieces. Combine next 8 ingredients and pour over the scallops. Turn occasionally for 3 hours. Serve with cocktails (use toothpicks).

Submitted by Bodine Ames, Vinalhaven, Maine

Scallop Stew

1 pound scallops
¼ cup butter
Salt and pepper to taste

½ tablespoon Worcestershire
    sauce
1 quart milk

Mélt the butter in a kettle, cut scallops into bite size pieces and add to the butter; add salt, pepper and Worcestershire sauce. Cook slowly until the scallops turn white, overcooking toughens fish. Scald the milk and add cooked scallops to it. Keep in mind a scallop stew is a little on the sweet side and also a rich stew.

Submitted by Nancie Bond, Jefferson, Maine

Scallop Stew

1½ cups fresh scallops
2 tablespoons butter or
    margarine

1 quart milk
½ teaspoon or more salt
Few grains cayenne pepper

If scallops are large, cut in small pieces. Cook the scallops lightly in the butter; too high a heat toughens the fish. Heat the milk in a double boiler; when hot, add the scallops and the butter in which they were cooked. Add salt and pepper. Cook the stew over hot water for 15 to 20 minutes. Taste for further seasoning.

Submitted by Mrs. W. E. Schrumpf, Orono, Maine

Scallop Casserole

1 pound scallops
1 (4 oz.) can mushrooms
1 (2 oz.) jar pimentos, sliced
sliced
¾ cup instant dry skim milk
1 small onion, sliced

3 tablespoons butter
2 tablespoons flour
1 teaspoon salt
2 cups liquid
Buttered crumbs

Parboil the scallops until just white in a small amount of water. Drain and save the liquid. To this liquid add liquid from the mushrooms and pimentos and enough water to make 2 cups. Stir into this the dry milk. Set aside. Fry the onion in butter until just golden, blend in flour and salt. Add the liquid gradually and cook, stirring until it thickens. Add scallops, mushrooms and pimentos. Pour into buttered baking dish. Cover with buttered crumbs and bake at 350 degrees until brown, about 20 minutes.

Submitted by Mrs. Carl Otto, Orono, Maine

Scallop Casserole

Scallops (1 pint)
Butter
1½ cups macaroni
1 can cream of mushroom soup

Milk
Small jar pimentos
½ bag frozen peas

Saute scallops in butter. Cook the 1½ cups macaroni or more if wanted. Mix together the soup, small amount of milk (enough to rinse out soup can), the pimentos and peas, combine with scallops. Put in buttered casserole and bake for about an hour in 350 degree oven.

Submitted by Goldie Chadwick, Thomaston, Maine

Scallop Casserole

1 pint scallops, cut up
1 cup cracker crumbs
½ cup soft bread crumbs

½ cup butter, melted
⅔ cup cream or top of milk
Salt and pepper to taste

Mix cracker crumbs and bread crumbs with melted butter (separately). Put scallops and bread crumbs in buttered casserole in alternate layers with the cracker crumbs on top. Salt and pepper. Add cream last and bake in 375 degree oven for 40 minutes.

Submitted by Elizabeth Shyne, Rockland, Maine

Scallop Casserole

1 pint Maine scallops
1 tablespoon diced green
    pepper
1 tablespoon onion, cut up
1 tablespoon butter
3 tablespoons flour

1 teaspoon dry mustard
1½ cups milk
1 cup grated cheese
½ can undiluted tomato soup
Few olives
Buttered crumbs

Cut scallops into quarters. Bring to a boil and cook slowly for 5 minutes. Drain. Cook green pepper and onion in the butter until tender. Add flour and mustard. Slowly add milk and cook until thickened. Add cheese, soup and olives. Mix with the drained scallops and place in buttered casserole. Top with buttered crumbs and bake at 350 degrees for 30 minutes.

Submitted by Mrs. J. Warren Everett, Thomaston, Maine

Scallop Casserole

2 tablespoons butter
Salt and pepper to taste
½ to ¾ cups bread crumbs
1 cup shredded Cheddar cheese
3 tablespoons sherry (optional)
1 pound scallops

½ cup light cream or evaporated
    milk

Melt butter in frying pan, add salt, pepper, crumbs, cheese and sherry. Mix with scallops or place scallops in buttered baking dish, pour cream and other mixture over it. Bake 30 to 35 minutes in 350 degree oven.

Submitted by Eleanor Foster, Warren, Maine

Scallop Casserole

½ pound scallops
½ pound haddock

1 can frozen shrimp soup,
    thawed
Buttered crumbs

Cut scallops into bite-size pieces and cook in a small amount of water for five minutes. Drain and place into a buttered casserole. Pour shrimp soup over the fish and cover with buttered crumbs. Bake 30 minutes at 350 degrees.

Submitted by Nancie Bond, Jefferson, Maine

Scallop Casserole

2 pounds scallops, cut in cubes
⅓ cup margarine
1 onion, chopped fine
⅓ cup flour
1½ teaspoons salt
½ teaspoon pepper
2½ cups milk
2 teaspoons dry mustard
2 teaspoons lemon juice
2 teaspoons parsley flakes
Buttered crumbs

Melt margarine in skillet, add onion and saute until tender. Stir in flour, salt and pepper, stir until well blended. Add milk and continue to stir until thickened. Blend in mustard, lemon juice and parsley flakes, stir until smooth. Add the cubed scallops. Pour into buttered casserole, top with buttered crumbs and bake 20 minutes at 350 degrees.

Submitted by Eleanor Clark, Thomaston, Maine

Fish Casserole

½ pound scallops
½ pound haddock
1 can frozen cream of shrimp soup
Buttered bread crumbs

Mix the scallops and haddock with the soup (undiluted). Put in buttered casserole. Top with buttered bread crumbs. Bake ¾ hour at 350 degrees.

Submitted by Mrs. Bernard Deering, Orono, Maine

Scalloped Scallops

1 pint scallops
3 tablespoons butter
2 teaspoons finely chopped onion
½ pound mushrooms, cut in small pieces
½ cup scallop liquor
1 cup cream
3 tablespoons flour
Salt, pepper and cayenne
Bread crumbs, buttered and seasoned

Parboil scallops. Drain and cut in pieces. Melt butter. Add onions and mushrooms. Cook 5 minutes. Add scallops and cook 5 more minutes. Add to this the liquids to which flour, salt, pepper and cayenne have been added and cook until thick. Place mixture in a buttered baking dish or scallop shells. Dot with butter. Cover with the bread crumbs. Bake until brown.

Submitted by Josephine C. Philbrick, Camden, Maine

Scalloped Scallops

1 pint scallops   Salt, pepper
½ cup butter   ¼ teaspoon prepared mustard
2 cups cracker crumbs   ½ cup milk

Mash the scallops or if large, cut up. Set aside. Melt butter and add it to the cracker crumbs. Cover the bottom of a baking dish with some of this mixture. Add a layer of scallops seasoned with salt, pepper and mustard. Add part of the milk. Repeat layers until dish is filled. Spread remaining cracker crumbs over top. Bake in moderate oven ½ hour.

Submitted by Mrs. Celia R. Adams, Thomaston, Maine

Scalloped Scallops

1 pint of scallops   1 cup milk
2 cups common cracker crumbs   Butter

Butter casserole dish. Put in layer of crumbs and layer of scallops alternately, ending with crumbs. Pour the milk over them and dot with butter. Bake in 350 degree oven about 30 minutes.

I have also used this for clams and used some of the clam water for part of the milk. Can also use soda crackers instead of the common.

Submitted by Mrs. Earl A. Wright, South Bristol, Maine

Scalloped Scallops

1 pint scallops   ½ cup soft bread crumbs
1 stick margarine   Salt and pepper
1 cup cracker crumbs   ⅔ cup milk or cream

Wash scallops and cut in pieces. Melt margarine and add to cracker and bread crumbs. Layer scallops and crumbs in casserole. Salt and pepper. Turn milk or cream over crumbs. Bake at 350 degrees for 30 minutes.

Submitted by Martha Wilson, Thomaston, Maine

41

SCALLOPED SCALLOPS are elegantly served in their own shells.
(Recipe on Page 40)

Escalloped Scallops

Scallops   ½ pound butter (for large dish)
Cracker crumbs   ½ pint cream

Take equal amounts of scallops, and cracker crumbs which
has been mixed with the butter. Put layer of crumbs and a layer
of scallops in casserole, cover with the cream and bake until
brown. Delicious.

Submitted by Charlotte C. Hopkins, Rockland, Maine

Escalloped Scallops

1 pint scallops   1 cup salted cracker crumbs
½ cup butter   ⅔ cup cream or top milk
Salt and pepper to taste

Melt the butter, add salt, pepper and cracker crumbs and mix
well. Put in layers with the scallops in buttered casserole, pour
cream over the top and bake at 350 degrees about 25 minutes.

Submitted by Mrs. Lucille Ray, Auburn, Maine

Cape Scallops Supreme

1 pound Cape scallops   1 dash pepper
½ cup cornmeal   1 dash parsley flakes
¼ teaspoon salt   Butter
1 tablespoon flour

Mix cornmeal, salt, flour, pepper and parsley flakes in a large
plastic or paper bag. Shake to mix. Put 6-8 scallops in bag at one
time. Shake to cover each scallop with cornmeal mix. Repeat
until all scallops are generously covered. Place scallops in shallow
baking dish or on a cookie sheet. Spread out side by side, dot with
butter. Place under broiler 4-5 minutes until golden brown, turning over at least once. Do not overcook. Scallops should be tender
and moist.

Submitted by John Alton Rose, New Sharon, Maine

Coquille Saint Jacques
(Real Fine Scallop Casserole)

1½ pounds scallops
2 sprigs fresh thyme or
2 teaspoons dried thyme
1 bay leaf
1 sprig parsley
8 peppercorns
Salt
½ cup water

½ cup dry white wine
7 tablespoons butter
3 tablespoons flour
2 egg yolks
1 teaspoon lemon juice
Cayenne pepper
Parmesan cheese

Combine scallops, thyme, bay leaf, parsley, peppercorns, salt, water and wine in a small pan and bring to a boil. Cover and simmer exactly 2 minutes. Remove parsley, bay leaf and thyme sprig and drain but reserve the cooking liquid. Let scallops cool (cut bay scallops in half or sea scallops into thin slices), set them aside. Melt 2 tablespoons butter and stir in the flour with a wire whisk. When blended add scallop liquid (about 1½ cups) stirring vigorously with whisk. Remove sauce from heat and beat with electric beater. Add remaining butter a little at a time, it must be added very gradually. Beat in egg yolks and continue beating until cool. Add lemon juice and cayenne. Put mixture and scallops into baking dish, sprinkle with Parmesan cheese. Bake 5 to 10 minutes until golden brown.

Submitted by Mrs. C. Gowing, Cushing, Maine

Scallop Cheese Pudding

6 slices of bread, buttered
1 package of large scallops
Salt and cayenne pepper
¼ to ½ pound Cheddar
cheese, chopped or grated

3 eggs, beaten slightly
½ teaspoon mustard
½ teaspoon paprika
1½ cups milk

Fit three slices of the bread into the bottom of a casserole dish. Cover with scallops, sprinkle with salt and cayenne pepper. Cover with the chopped or grated cheese, add rest of the bread, scallops, cheese, and season as before. Beat eggs slightly, add milk, mustard and paprika. Add more salt (to taste). Bake in a 350 degree oven for 30 minutes or until scallops are done.

Submitted by Carrie S. Libby, Palmyra, Maine

Deviled Scallops

1 pint scallops
½ teaspoon salt
¼ teaspoon pepper
⅓ cup flour
¼ cup butter, melted

1 cup milk
1 egg, beaten
1 tablespoon lemon juice
Buttered crumbs

Pour boiling water over scallops and let stand 3 to 5 minutes. Drain and cut smaller if scallops are large. Mix the salt, pepper and flour together and add to the melted butter, mix to smooth paste. Heat the milk and add to the flour mixture, add beaten egg and lemon juice. Stir this into the scallops. Put in casserole, cover with buttered crumbs and bake in moderately hot oven until crumbs are browned.

Submitted by Mrs. Wm. D. Murphy, Jr., Elliot, Maine

Baked Scallops Maine

2 pounds scallops
1 slice lemon
1 tablespoon chopped parsley
7 tablespoons butter
1 tablespoon chopped onions
½ pound sliced mushrooms

3 tablespoons flour
Worcestershire sauce
Salt, pepper
¼ cup sherry
¼ cup buttered bread crumbs
4 tablespoons grated cheese

Wash scallops quickly in cold water; wipe dry. If they are large cut in half across the grain. Place in a saucepan, cover with cold water, add lemon and parsley. Boil 2 minutes. Drain scallops; strain liquid and reserve.

Melt 4 tablespoons butter in frying pan; saute onions and mushrooms until onions are tender.

Melt remaining 3 tablespoons butter in a saucepan; add flour and blend. Slowly add the liquid from the scallops, a dash of Worcestershire sauce, salt and pepper, stirring continuously. When mixture is smooth, add the scallops, sauteed onions, mushrooms, and sherry.

Place in a well-buttered baking dish; sprinkle with buttered crumbs and cheese. Bake in moderate oven (350 degrees) 10 to 15 minutes.

Makes 6 servings.

I serve this with green salad, rice and popovers with something good and sweet for dessert. *Just right.*

Submitted by Deborah Gorman, Waldoboro, Maine

Mother's Baked Scallops

Flour   Butter
Scallops   Hot Water
Salt, pepper   Milk

Cut the scallops once or twice. Put a little flour in a pan and cover with a layer of scallops, sprinkle again with flour, salt and pepper. Dot with butter. Add a little hot water and bake 20 to 30 minutes. When most done, add a little milk.

Submitted by Clara W. Thornton, North Haven, Maine

Seafood Continental

4 cups drained, cooked   2 tablespoons dry white wine
   seafood (crab, lobster,   (optional)
   shrimp, whitefish)   1 cup shredded mild cheese
2 cans cream of celery soup   2 tablespoons parsley
⅓ to ½ cup water   ¼ cup buttered bread crumbs

Blend soup, water and wine. Mix with the combination of seafood, cheese and parsley. Spoon seafood mixture into shallow baking dish 10"x6"x2". Top with the buttered crumbs. Bake at 400 degrees for about 20 minutes.

Submitted by Mrs. Austin W. Miller, Friendship, Maine

Seafood Supreme

2 cups scallops, cut bite-size   1 cup evaporated milk
½ cup water   2 teaspoons paprika
1 pound haddock   1 teaspoon Worcestershire
2 cups shrimp (2 medium cans)   sauce
½ cup butter   Dash cayenne pepper
½ cup flour

Simmer scallops in the ½ cup water. Melt butter in double boiler. Add flour, milk and liquid from the scallops, cook until thick. Add paprika, sauce and cayenne pepper and cook 10 minutes over medium heat. Now add the scallops, haddock and shrimp and cook 25 minutes. Will serve 6.

Submitted by Mary W. Sibo, Old Town, Maine

Fish Chowder

1 pound scallops, cut up
3 pounds haddock, cut up
1 large tin of frozen lobster,
  cut up
½ pound cubed salt pork
2 medium onions, cut up
4 cups water

6 cups diced potatoes
¼ pound butter
4 teaspoons salt
4 teaspoons chopped parsley
½ teaspoon curry powder
2 quarts milk
1 large can evaporated milk

Melt salt pork, add onions and cook, but do not brown. Add water and potatoes and cook 10 minutes. Add scallops and when almost cooked add haddock and cook a few minutes more. Now add the frozen lobster, butter, salt, parsley and curry powder. Let stand overnight. In the morning add the 2 milks. Will serve 25.

Submitted by Mrs. F. C. Fisher, Rothesay, New Brunswick

Seafood Chowder

¼ cup margarine
¼ cup minced onion
2 cups finely diced raw potato
½ pound fresh scallops
½ pound fresh haddock
1 cup water (more may be needed)

2 cups milk
1 can shrimp

Saute onion in margarine. Add potatoes, fish and water. Cook until tender (more water may be needed). Add milk and shrimp. Heat to serving, but do not boil.

Submitted by Margaret Salsbury, Otis, Maine

Breaded Scallops

Scald the scallops well. Drain and dust with salt and pepper. Dip in melted butter, roll in fine dry bread crumbs, sprinkle with lemon juice and add more salt and pepper if liked. Bake or broil until golden brown.

Submitted by Lulu M. Miller, Waldoboro, Maine

Oven-Fried Scallops

1 pound (1½ cups) scallops	2 tablespoons water
Salt and pepper to taste	¾ cup fine dry crumbs
1 egg	¼ cup butter, melted

Wipe scallops dry, then sprinkle with salt and pepper. Beat egg and water together. Dip scallops in egg mixture, dry crumbs and then in melted butter. Place in shallow baking dish. Bake at 450 degrees for 25 minutes.

Submitted by Mary Richards Wiley, Tenants Harbor, Maine

Scallop Fritters

1 egg	½ teaspoon salt
½ cup milk	Pepper
1¼ cups flour	Scallops
2 teaspoons baking powder	

Beat egg thoroughly, add milk. Sift dry ingredients and mix with the egg, milk mixture stirring with a wooden spoon to make a smooth batter. Dry scallops, sprinkle lightly with salt and pepper. Dip in the batter, drain quickly and immerse in hot fat. Fry 2 minutes 380 degrees. Drain and serve.

Submitted by Leland C. Foster, Wiscasset, Maine

Canning Shrimp

1 cup salt
1 cup vinegar

To each gallon boiling water needed for cooking shrimp. Wash and drain freshly caught shrimp. Drop into boiling brine. Boil 10 minutes, drop into cold water. Drain and peel, Remove sand vein, rinse in cold water. Pack in hot pint jars, leaving 1 inch head space. Adjust caps. Process 45 minutes at 10 pounds pressure.

Submitted by Mrs. Stella Brooks, Bath, Maine

Baked Stuffed Shrimp

1 package raw frozen shrimp
  (thawed)
¼ cup chopped onion
¼ cup chopped green pepper

3 tablespoons butter
1 cup seasoned stuffing
Melted butter

Saute onion and green pepper in butter (3 tbsp.). Add the seasoned stuffing and toss together with onion and pepper until coated with butter. In a buttered 9-inch oven-proof pie plate put the shrimp. Sprinkle the dressing on top of shrimp. It will be like a crumb topping. Pour melted butter over topping and bake at 450 degrees for 5 to 8 minutes. Serves 2.

Submitted by Christine McMahon, Rockland, Maine

Baked Shrimp

1 pound shrimp
1 cup cracker crumbs

¼ cup butter

Place shrimp in a single layer on a baking sheet. Cover with cracker crumbs and butter. Bake at 375 degrees for 15 minutes.

Submitted by Mrs. Eugene Doran, Rockland, Maine

Baked Stuffed Shrimp

1 pound frozen clean shrimp
1 box (12 oz.) salted crackers
1 can minced clams
1 small can mushrooms,
  chopped

¼ to ½ pound butter,
melted Paprika

49   continued

Cut up three of the shrimp in small pieces. Crush the crackers. Mix together well the small pieces of shrimp, crackers, clams, mushrooms and part of the melted butter. Line 4 small oven-proof dishes or 1 casserole dish with half of the crumb mixture. Put whole shrimp on top then add remaining crumbs. Drizzle butter over this and sprinkle with paprika. Bake 10 minutes at 450 degrees then 10 more minutes in a 350 degree oven. Turn oven off and let stand 10 minutes with door open. Serves 4.

Submitted by Barbara B. Hutchins, Jefferson, Maine

Creamed Shrimp On Biscuits

½ cup butter
Flour
Salt, pepper, paprika
1 tablespoon sherry

1½ cups milk
1½ pounds cooked shrimp
Hot biscuits

Melt butter, add enough flour to thicken. Add salt, pepper, paprika and sherry. Slowly add the milk to make a cream sauce. When smooth, add shrimp and serve over hot split biscuits. (Also a yummy sauce to mix thin and pour over fish fillets with stuffing baked on them.)

Submitted by Bodine Ames, Vinalhaven, Maine

Shrimp Custard Pie

1 unbaked 10-inch pie shell
1 pound cooked shrimp, cut up
2 tablespoons bacon bits (or 4 slices bacon cooked and crumbled)
1 cup chopped pimento
2 cups milk

4 eggs
⅓ cup grated Parmesan cheese
½ teaspoon salt
¼ teaspoon thyme
Dash of hot pepper sauce

Place cut-up shrimp in pie shell and sprinkle with bacon bits and pimento. In mixing bowl beat eggs with milk, cheese, salt, thyme and pepper sauce. Pour over shrimp mixture and bake at 375 degrees for 35 to 40 minutes or until a knife inserted near center comes out clean. Let stand 10 minutes before serving. Serves 8.

Submitted by Elizabeth H. Cutliffe, North Edgecomb, Maine

Sunset Shrimp Casserole

Buttered slices of bread
Cheese slices
Shrimp
Buttered crumbs
2 eggs

1 teaspoon salt
½ teaspoon dry mustard
Dash of cayenne
Milk

Place buttered slices of bread in bottom of casserole, on this a layer of cheese slices and then a layer of shrimp. Make these three layers to amount desired. Place more cheese slices on top, then buttered crumbs. Beat eggs with salt, mustard and a dash of cayenne if desired. Add milk to nearly cover and bake at 325 degrees about an hour.

Submitted by Ruth Bond, Jefferson, Maine

Shrimp Casserole

2 cups shrimp, fresh or
  canned
1⅓ cups minute rice
2 cans mushroom soup
1 cup milk

1 green pepper, diced
Parsley flakes
Salt and pepper to taste
Buttered crumbs

Mix all together (except crumbs) in a casserole. Cover with the crumbs. Bake 25 minutes in a 350 degree oven.

Submitted by Norma Clark, Rockland, Maine

Shrimp Casserole

1 cup butter or margarine,
  melted
⅓ cup chopped parsley
⅔ cup cooking sherry
2 cups soft bread crumbs

2 cloves garlic, minced
½ teaspoon paprika
Dash cayenne
5 to 6 cups cleaned and cooked
  shrimp (2 large packages)

51

continued

To the melted butter add parsley, sherry, bread crumbs, garlic, paprika and cayenne. Mix well. Put shrimp in a 11x7 shallow dish. Spoon batter over the shrimp and bake at 325 degrees for 25 minutes. Serves 6 to 8.

Submitted by Mrs. Anne DeRoche, Lisbon Falls, Maine

Shrimp Casserole

4 ounces (3 cups) medium
  noodles
1 can frozen shrimp soup
¾ cup milk
¼ cup diced celery
1 tablespoon chopped onion

¼ teaspoon salt
⅓ cup shredded Cheddar
  cheese
2 cups cooked shrimp
¼ cup chow mein noodles

Cook the noodles. Thaw the soup and combine with milk, celery, onion and salt. Mix well. Stir in cheese, shrimp and cooked noodles. Pour into 1½-quart casserole and bake uncovered at 350 degrees for 30 minutes. Top with chow mein noodles last 10 minutes of baking.

Submitted by Julia Burgess, Waldoboro, Maine

Shrimp Casserole

2 packages of frozen chopped
  broccoli
1 pound Maine frozen shrimp
Salt, pepper, monosodium
  glutamate
1 can celery soup
1 cup mayonnaise

1 teaspoon lemon juice
½ cup Cheddar cheese,
  (shredded)
Herb bread crumbs
Melted butter

Grease a shallow casserole and place chopped broccoli in the bottom with the frozen shrimp on top. Sprinkle with salt, pepper and monosodium glutamate. Mix soup with mayonnaise, lemon juice, and cheese. Pour over mixture in casserole. Mix bread crumbs with melted butter and put on top. Bake in a 350 degree oven about 30 minutes.

Submitted by Mrs. E. Ashley Walter, Jr., Waldoboro, Maine

Shrimp Casserole

1 can mushrooms (medium button)
2 cans mushroom soup
1 can chopped celery (use soup can to measure)
1 can chopped onion
1 package frozen shrimp (1 pound or more)

1 package frozen lobster bits (1 pound)
¼ cup water
1 No. 2 can Chinese noodles (save ¼ can for topping)
6 ounces cashew nuts (chopped)
Melted butter

Combine all ingredients in a baking dish and sprinkle on top the ¼ can of noodles and drizzle with melted butter. Bake for 30 minutes in a 350 degree oven. We serve this casserole with rice or mixed wild rice and white. Delicious and very attractive served in a fish-shaped dish.

Submitted by Gladys E. Philbrick, Rockland, Maine

Rice And Shrimp Casserole

3 cups cooked rice
1 pound cooked shrimp
1 can tomatoes
1 green pepper, chopped

2 teaspoons salt
Garlic powder or savory, optional

Combine all ingredients. Bake at 350 degrees about 35 minutes. Can be made ahead and refrigerated. 4 servings.

Submitted by Ruth Bond, Jefferson, Maine

Shrimp-Eggplant Casserole

½ cup chopped onion
¼ cup chopped green pepper
½ cup chopped parsley (fresh)
⅓ cup margarine
1 large eggplant
⅔ cup water
1 cup canned tomatoes

1 teaspoon salt
½ teaspoon crushed thyme
1 garlic clove, chopped fine
2 bay leaves
¾ pound cooked Maine shrimp (shelled)
2 tablespoons margarine
¾ cup dry bread crumbs

53

continued

Cook onions, pepper and parsley in margarine until tender. Pare and cook eggplant until tender and drain. To eggplant pulp, add tomatoes, seasonings, then add to onion mixture and simmer for 10 minutes. Remove bay leaves and add shrimp. Combine the bread crumbs and the 2 tablespoons margarine. Place alternate layers of eggplant and shrimp mixture and the crumbs in a buttered casserole. Top with crumbs. Bake at 400 degrees for about 35 minutes.

Submitted by Irma W. Benner, South Harpswell, Maine

Shrimp And Mushroom Casserole

2 pounds cooked shrimp
6 tablespoons butter
1 pound mushrooms (thinly sliced)
Salt, pepper, dash of nutmeg

1 cup light cream
½ cup crushed salted crackers
Flour
Paprika

In 4 tablespoons of the butter, saute mushrooms for 3 minutes. Lift out and place in the bottom of a shallow baking dish. Stir flour, salt, pepper and nutmeg into the drippings in the skillet until smooth. Stir in the light cream, bring to a boil and add the shrimp. Spoon shrimp mixture over the mushrooms in the baking dish. Melt the rest of the butter and mix with cracker crumbs. Sprinkle over the top and lightly dust with paprika. Bake uncovered for about 30 minutes or until bubbly hot, in a 300 degree oven.

Submitted by Jeannette Chapman, Cushing, Maine

Seafood Casserole For 35 To 40 Servings

2 pounds Maine shrimp
3 pounds haddock
2 pounds Maine scallops
2 pounds Maine crabmeat
½ pound margarine
1½ cups flour
6 cups milk and 2 cups fish cooking liquid

3 cups cream
2 tablespoons salt
½ teaspoon cayenne pepper
½ cup sherry (optional)
2½ cups herb-seasoned stuffing mix or buttered crumbs

Parboil haddock and scallops until tender, 15 minutes or less; reserve the cooking liquid. Remove any bones from the haddock. Make a sauce of the margarine, flour, pepper, salt, milk, fish liquid and cream. When smooth and thickened, add the fish, scallops, shrimp (uncooked), crabmeat and sherry. Taste for further seasoning. Spoon mixture into buttered casseroles and top with herb seasoned stuffing mix or prepare your own buttered herb seasoned crumbs. Bake in a 325 degree oven for 1 hour or until hot and bubbly.

Submitted by Mildred Brown Schrumpf, Orono, Maine

Seven Seas Casserole

1 can cream of mushroom soup
1¼ cups milk
¼ teaspoon salt
1⅓ cups minute rice
  (uncooked)
Paprika

½ pound seafood (cooked),
  usually shrimp
1 box frozen peas (thawed
  but not cooked)
Cheese slices

Mix soup, milk and salt in a saucepan. Bring to a slow boil. Pour half of this mixture into a greased 1½-quart casserole. Then in layers add rice, peas, seafood, then the rest of the soup. Top with cheese slices. Sprinkle with paprika. Bake at 375 degrees for 30 minutes. Serves 4.

Submitted by Mrs. Harry Stewart, Union, Maine

Seafood Casserole

1 cup rice (uncooked)
1 pound shrimp or less
1 can (7 or 8 oz.) crabmeat
1 can frozen shrimp soup

1 can newburg sauce
  or
½ cup sherry and milk

Cook rice, add shrimp, crabmeat and soup. Use the newburg sauce to thin the shrimp soup or use the sherry and milk. Pour into a well greased casserole. Cover with seasoned buttered crumbs. Bake at 350 degrees about ½ hour or until bubbly.

This is a very versatile recipe. If shrimp are plentiful and crabmeat is too expensive, it is delicious made entirely with shrimp. You may also use canned shrimp soup or mushroom soup to make it less expensive. I usually use the sherry and milk to just thin the soup that I'm using. I find it is a simple recipe for church or other potluck suppers and it is well liked.

Submitted by Alice N. Merry, North Edgecomb, Maine

Five Islands Shrimp Casserole

1 cup cut-up celery
1 cup onions, cut-up
1 cup green peppers, diced
3 tablespoons butter or
   margarine
1 pound thawed shrimps
1 tablespoon soy sauce

2 tablespoons flour
1/2 cup water
1 tablespoon curry powder
Salt and pepper to taste
1/2 cup crushed pineapple
1 sliced banana
Fluffy rice

Saute celery, onions and green pepper until tender, and add 1 cup of water. Add the thawed shrimp and soy sauce. Cook for 5 minutes. Add the 2 tablespoons of flour to the 1/2 cup of water, mix well and add to the shrimp-vegetable mixture with the curry powder, salt and pepper. Just before serving, add pineapple and banana. Serve on fluffy rice.

Submitted by Marion Watson, Five Islands, Maine

Shrimp Potato Stew

2 cups raw potatoes, sliced
2 cups water
1 pint raw shrimp

2 cups milk
Butter
Salt to taste

Boil potatoes in the water until almost tender. Add shrimp and boil until the potatoes are cooked. Now add milk and heat as for stew. Add butter and salt to taste.

Submitted by Evelyn C. Roberts, Damariscotta, Maine

Quick Shrimp Curry

1/2 cup chopped onion
1 tablespoon butter or margarine
1 can frozen cream of shrimp
   soup
1 cup dairy sour cream
1/2 teaspoon curry powder or
   paprika

1 cup cleaned, cooked or
   frozen shrimp
3 cups cooked rice (1 cup
   raw rice)

Cook onions in butter or margarine until tender but not browned. Add the soup, heat and stir until smooth. Stir in sour cream and curry powder, add shrimp and heat. Sprinkle with paprika and serve over hot rice.

Submitted by Rose L. Wales, Cushing, Maine

SHRIMP CURRY, surrounding a mound of molded rice and served with assorted condiments, lends an exotic touch to a buffet meal. (Recipe on Page 56)

Shrimp Curry With Noodles

1 package (7 oz.) shrimp curry with noodles
1 package (7 oz.) frozen shrimp
2 tablespoons butter
2 tablespoons instant minced onion
1½ teaspoons curry powder
1 can (10½ oz.) cream of mushroom soup
1 cup evaporated milk
1 can (5 oz.) chow mein noodles

Cook shrimp according to package directions. Drain. Melt the butter over low heat; stir in onion and curry powder. Remove from heat and stir in soup, mixing well. Slowly blend in the evaporated milk. Return to low heat and heat to serving temperature, stirring constantly. Add shrimp and cook, stirring for ½ minute longer. Serve over heated chow mein noodles. Makes 4 servings.

Submitted by Margaret Jenny, Belgrade, Maine

Shrimp Creole

4 tablespoons butter
1 cup chopped onion
1 cup chopped celery
½ cup green pepper
3 cloves garlic, minced, or
⅜ teaspoon instant minced garlic
2½ cups diced tomatoes
3 tablespoons parsley
1 teaspoon salt
¼ teaspoon cayenne pepper
3 bay leaves
3 cups cold water
4 tablespoons flour, mixed in cold water
1 can (12 oz.) tomato paste
2 pounds Maine frozen shrimp

Melt butter in saucepan. Saute onion, celery and green pepper until soft, about 5 minutes. Remove pan from direct heat and slowly stir in flour and water mixture. Add parsley, bay leaves, garlic, salt, cayenne pepper, tomatoes and tomato sauce. Simmer 15 minutes. Add Maine frozen shrimp, cover and simmer 25-30 minutes. Serve over cooked fluffy rice. Serves 6-8 people.

Submitted by Marilyn M. Wiers, St. Albans, Maine

Sweet And Pungent Shrimp

1 pound shrimp (fresh or
  frozen)
2 eggs, beaten
½ cup flour
1 green pepper, sliced
1 can (15 oz.) pineapple
  chunks and juice
½ cup vinegar
⅔ cup sugar

½ teaspoon monosodium
  glutamate
½ cup water
½ teaspoon salt
3 teaspoons cornstarch mixed
  with water
1 tablespoon soy sauce
Rice

If using fresh shrimp, boil for 3 to 5 minutes in rapidly boiling salted water (1 tbsp. salt per quart of water), shell and devein.
If using frozen shrimp follow directions on package.
Beat eggs with the flour and add shrimp. Stir to coat shrimp well. Fry in salad oil to a delicate brown. Remove shrimp from the pan and add green pepper, pineapple chunks and juice, vinegar, sugar, monosodium glutamate, water, salt, and cornstarch mixed with water. Stir and cook for about 10 minutes. Then add soy sauce and shrimp. Cook another 2 minutes. Serve with boiled rice. Just as good warmed over the next day.

Submitted by Mrs. Carl Otto, Orono, Maine

French Fried Shrimp

1 cup flour
1 teaspoon baking powder
½ teaspoon salt
⅔ cup milk
1 egg

1 tablespoon corn oil
1½ pounds shrimp (shelled
  and deveined)
1 quart corn oil

Combine flour, baking powder and salt. Mix together the milk, egg and tablespoon corn oil. Add to flour mixture. Stir until smooth. Dip shrimp in batter. Drain well. Pour corn oil into heavy, sturdy, flat-bottomed 3-quart saucepan, filling utensil no more than ⅓ full. Heat over medium heat to 375 degrees. Carefully add shrimp, a few at a time. Fry 2 to 3 minutes or until golden brown. Serves 6.

Submitted by Donna Bond, Jefferson, Maine

Eastern Fried Shrimp

1½ pounds raw shrimp
½ cup lemon juice
1 cup all purpose flour

3 eggs, beaten
1½ teaspoons salt
Dash of pepper

Shell and devein the shrimp. Pour lemon juice over shrimp and let set for 15 minutes. Cut shrimp down back to last tail section, spread out butterfly style. Place flour in a bag and add shrimp. Toss to coat shrimp well with flour. Combine eggs, salt and pepper. Dip each shrimp in egg. Heat about ⅛ inch of fat in a skillet, and when hot, drop in enough shrimp to cover bottom. Brown on both sides. Remove and add more shrimp. Cook about 4 minutes. Drain on absorbent paper. This recipe should serve 6 people but it is so good it may only do for four.
Submitted by Mrs. Estelle K. Anderson, Tenants Harbor, Maine

Shrimp Fritters

2 cups pancake mix
2 cups milk

2 eggs, beaten
Raw shrimp meat

Beat eggs, stir in milk and pancake mix. Cut shrimp meat into small pieces, whatever amount you like, and add to mix. Fry slowly in medium hot skillet until done.
Submitted by Mrs. Shirley Yattaw, Rockland, Maine

Shrimp Dip

¾ cup mayonnaise
1 teaspoon tomato puree
1 teaspoon cognac

Chopped chives
Shrimps

Stir together the first 3 ingredients, sprinkle with chopped chives. Serve with shrimps as dip.
Submitted by Eleanor C. Linton, Camden, Maine

Pink Shrimp Dip

6 ounces cream cheese
⅓ cup salad dressing or mayonnaise
3 tablespoons chili sauce

2 teaspoons lemon juice
½ teaspoon onion juice
½ teaspoon Worcestershire sauce
1 cup cooked shrimp, cut up

Blend cream cheese with the seasonings. Mix in the shrimp. Serve with crackers, chips, etc.

Submitted by Elizabeth H. Cutliffe, North Edgecomb, Maine

Shrimp Rice Bake

4 slices bread, buttered and cubed
2 cups boiled rice
1 can stewed tomatoes (with onions, celery and green peppers)
1 can condensed Cheddar cheese soup

1 teaspoon parsley flakes
1 teaspoon minced green onions
1 to 1½ cups cooked Maine shrimp (shelled)

Saute the bread and butter over very low heat in a pan until dry and reserve for top.

Cook rice in saucepan until done and no water left (cook as to directions on rice package for 2 cups). In same saucepan add the tomato mixture, undiluted soup, parsley and minced onion and heat altogether over medium heat, stirring constantly until the cheese soup melts and blends and mixture is bubbly. Then add the shrimp. Pour mixture into greased 1½ quart casserole and put buttered crumbs on top. Bake in 375 degree oven until browned.

Submitted by Irma W. Benner, South Harpswell

Shrimp Wiggle

1 pound shrimp meat or 1 can shrimp
4 tablespoons butter
4 tablespoons flour

2 cups milk
½ teaspoon salt
Dash of pepper
1 cup canned peas

Make a white sauce of butter, flour and milk. Season with salt and pepper. Add shrimp and the peas, heat thoroughly. Serve on toast or crackers.

Submitted by Martha Wilson, Thomaston, Maine

Seafood Newburg

½ cup butter or margarine
3 tablespoons flour
2 cups light cream or
  half-in-half
4 egg yolks, slightly beaten
⅔ teaspoon salt
1 cup cleaned cooked shrimp
  or ¾ pound shrimp in shells

1 pound crabmeat or 2 lobster
  tails, cooked
⅓ cup cooking sherry
2 teaspoons lemon juice
Paprika

Note: You can substitute 2 cans of frozen shrimp soup in place of fresh shrimp. Dilute soup with 1 cup cream or half-in-half. Also in place of crabmeat you can use ½ pound haddock and 1 pound scallops.

Melt butter in chafing dish. Blend flour in half-in-half. Cook slowly until thickened. Stir small amount of sauce in egg yolks. Return to skillet or chafing dish, stirring constantly for about 1 minute. Add salt, shrimp, and crabmeat. Heat slowly. Add sherry and lemon juice. Sprinkle with paprika. Serve on toast points or in patty shells. Will yield 8 servings. An excellent luncheon dish.

Submitted by Helen C. Loose, Camden, Maine

Shrimp On Toast

1 pound raw Maine shrimp,
  cleaned
5 water chestnuts
2 strips of bacon

1 teaspoon salt
1 tablespoon dry sherry
Bread (day old)
1 quart oil

Chop shrimp, chestnuts and bacon together. Add salt and sherry and mix to form a paste. Trim crust from the bread and spread the shrimp paste (about 1 heaping tablespoon on each slice. Fry in hot oil, first shrimp side down until brown, then the other side.

Submitted by Dolores Reglin, Orrington, Maine

Jellied Seafood Salad

2 cups canned tomatoes or
  1½ cups tomato juice
½ bay leaf
¾ cup chopped celery
2 teaspoons grated onion
½ teaspoon salt
Dash cayenne

1 envelope unflavored gelatin
¼ cup cold water
1 tablespoon lemon juice
2 tablespoons chopped green
  pepper
1 cup Maine shrimp,* diced

Mix tomatoes, bay leaf, ¼ cup of celery, onion, salt and cayenne; simmer 10 minutes; strain. Soften gelatin in cold water; dissolve in hot tomato stock, add lemon juice. Chill until slightly thickened. Fold in green pepper, remaining celery and the shrimp (reserve 9 shrimp for garnish). Place the whole shrimp on bottom of mold. Spoon salad mixture carefully into mold so as not to disturb garnish. Chill until firm. Unmold, garnish with mounds of cole slaw; serve with mayonnaise or salad dressing. Serves 6.
*Other fish or shellfish may be used.
Submitted by Marilyn M. Wiers, St. Albans, Maine

Squid

The squid is an unusual shellfish. The compact internal shell or quill sets this mollusk apart from other shellfish, which have external armor. When properly prepared, squid rivals such delicacies as scallops and lobster in flavor.

Your local fish dealer will gladly clean the squid for you, or if you're adventurous, try it yourself. Simply hold the squid body in your right hand, grip the head and tentacles with your left hand and firmly but gently pull apart. If done correctly, all contents of the sac will come away attached to the tentacles. Clean out the body cavity, rinsing well in cold water, and remove the cellophane-like quill.

The tentacles are excellent sauteed. Cut them off just in front of the eyes, discarding the head. Peel off the skin and dry on paper towels.

Those who object to the squid's appearance, whole, are amazed at the glistening white meat it produces when skinned and cut into fillets or rings.

Squid With Tomatoes
(Colomai con Pomadore)

2 pounds squid
4 tablespoons olive oil
½ onion sliced, small
2 garlic cloves
2 tablespoons minced fresh
  parsley

1 cup tomatoes
½ cup sherry (dry)
Salt and pepper to taste
Pinch oregano

Clean squid thoroughly. Remove outside skin, eyes and intestines. Clean skin off of the tentacles and cut body into 1 inch rings. Saute onion with olive oil and garlic, and brown. Add squid, cover and saute for 10 minutes. Add salt, pepper, sherry and oregano. Cook for 10 minutes over low heat without cover. This will allow the liquid to cook off. Add tomatoes (crushed between the fingers) and parsley. Cook for another 20 minutes.

Serve hot with Italian bread and butter. Serves 4 to 6. (May add a bit of hot pepper if desired.)

Submitted by Dr. A. Amaltifano, Waterville, Maine
Through courtesy of Mrs. Laura Cifala, Arlington, Virginia

Stuffed Squid

8 small squid
1 small chopped onion
2 tablespoons olive oil
2 cloves minced garlic
2 tablespoons minced fresh

parsley
1½ cups bread crumbs
½ cup grated Parmesan
  cheese
Salt and pepper

Clean squid thoroughly; remove eyes, intestines and outside skin (under running cold water). Drain. Chop up tentacles, saute in olive oil with onions and minced garlic. Remove from heat, and add bread crumbs, cheese, parsley, salt and pepper. Fill the cavity of each squid with above stuffing, fasten with toothpicks. Place in a baking pan and cover with the following:

1 can (No. 2) tomatoes
4 tablespoons olive oil

1 garlic clove

Brown the garlic in olive oil, mash tomatoes and add. Simmer for 20 minutes. Pour over the squid and bake in a 400 degree oven for 35 minutes. Serve whole with the sauce.

May also be served over cooked linguini. Sprinkle with Parmesan cheese, if desired. Serves 4.

Submitted by Dr. A. Amaltifano, Waterville, Maine
Through courtesy of Mrs. Laura Cifala, Arlington, Virginia

SEAFOOD STEW is even better the second day! (Recipe on Page 76)

Saltwater Fish

In the early days of commercial fishing, hand-lining was quickly superseded by hand-tub trawling. This method called for vigorous activities by the fishermen who were constantly at work from the time the trawler neared the fishing banks until they headed for home.

The trawl lines were laid from dories carried aboard the trawlers. The lines were allowed to set for 45 minutes and then were hauled in with as many as 600 pounds of fish. The mother ship picked up all of the dories, after which the fish were dressed and packed in ice. This type of fishing was very hazardous, and many times men who had drifted from the mother ship were forced to row as much as 175 miles to shore. Unfortunately, there were many fishermen who never made it.

Today the vessels are mostly steel-hulled with large holds, capable of carrying and sometimes processing many tons of fish. These vessels are propelled by diesel engines and equipped with numerous devices for communicating with the shore and other ships, as well as detecting the presence of fish beneath the surface of water.

As a result of newer methods of fishing, it is no longer the hit-or-miss proposition it was even 25 years ago. Fish are caught more readily and are taken to the processing plant far more quickly. Improved methods of handling and processing, both on board and ashore, have resulted in a high quality of unsurpassed food.

However, in spite of the most modern equipment, the battle with the sea has never ended. Every time a storm lashes the ocean into a fury, fishermen must fight for their lives, and every year the sea takes its ruthless toll of men and ships.

Seafoods from the pure cool waters just off the coast of Maine are of very high quality. They have a fine delicious texture that is to be found nowhere else.

Saltwater fish are just as sweet and free from salt as those caught in rivers and lakes. Saltwater fish just are not salty.

Recipes for cooking these delicacies have been passed down for generations from mothers to daughters.

The fame of these Atlantic fish has been spread far and wide by the many visitors to Maine every year. Among the former are to be found alewives, cod, cusk, flounder, haddock, hake, halibut, herring (sea), mackerel, ocean perch, pollock, Atlantic salmon, shad, smelt, squid, tuna, and whiting.

Bluefish

Bluefish, also called snapper or skipjack, is one of the popular saltwater game fish of the Atlantic Coast. It is a long slim and sort of greenish-blue fish. The average size is from 5 to 12 pounds, but a 25-pound one was caught off Massachusetts coast. It is a nomadic species and ranges from Nova Scotia to Brazil, with sometimes as many as 40 years between migrational swings. Anglers get them from shore in the surf and from boats, using menhaden for bait or artificial lures. More than 6 million pounds are caught by commercial fisheries annually.

Baked Bluefish

½ a whole fish or fillets
½ cup Italian salad dressing
1 cup hot water

Bread crumbs, Italian bread or
   white bread

Spread fish in an 8x10 pan, not layered. Mix salad dressing with hot water and pour over the fish. Cover with bread crumbs. Bake uncovered in a 350 degree oven for 25 to 30 minutes or until fish flakes easily. Do not grease pan or add any fat as this fish is rather oily. Serve with baked potatoes and a green salad.

Submitted by Mrs. Jeremiah Jellison, Bar Harbor, Maine

Bluefish And Potato Casserole

2 cups boiled, flaked bluefish
4 cups boiled, sliced potatoes
⅓ cup grated or finely diced onion
1 can cream of mushroom soup

1⅓ cups milk
1 teaspoon poultry seasoning
Salt and pepper
Crumbs

Place 2 cups of the potato in a 2-quart casserole (greased). Sprinkle half of onion on potato and add bluefish, then the rest of the onion and the rest of the potato. Mix mushroom soup with the milk and stir in seasoning. Pour over the ingredients in casserole. Dot with butter and sprinkle with crumbs or crushed cereal. Bake in a 375 degree oven for 35 to 40 minutes.

Submitted by Olga Burkett, Thomaston, Maine

Bluefish With Stuffing

1½ cups bread crumbs
¼ cup milk
1 or 2 teaspoons grated raw onion

½ teaspoon salt
¼ teaspoon grated lemon rind
1 teaspoon melted margarine
1 medium-sized bluefish

Mix ingredients well and stuff the fish. Place in an 8 x 10 baking dish and bake in a 350 degree oven about 30 to 35 minutes or until done. Can use onion soup mix in place of raw onion. It is an oily fish so needs no added fat.

Submitted by Mrs. Hazel Hills, Warren, Maine

Broiled Bluefish

Bluefish slices (cut crosswise)
Milk
Crumbs (bread or cracker)

Beaten egg
Salt and pepper

Mix milk, beaten egg, salt and pepper. Dip slices in milk-egg mixture and in crumbs. Broil or fry until done and well browned. As this is an oily fish, very little fat is needed.

Submitted by Ruth Russell, Rockland, Maine

Bluefish Macaroni Casserole

1½ cups boiled, flaked bluefish
4 cups cooked macaroni
¼ cup grated onion
2 hard-cooked eggs
1 can Cheddar cheese soup

1½ cups milk
1 teaspoon salt
Dash pepper (optional)
Bread crumbs (or any other kind)

Using a 2-quart buttered casserole, put half of the macaroni in the bottom. Slice one egg over macaroni, add a little onion and the bluefish, the rest of the macaroni and onion and slice the other egg over this. Mix cheese soup and milk with salt and pepper. Pour over mixture in casserole, dot with butter and cover with crumbs. Bake for 30 to 35 minutes in 350 degree oven.

Submitted by Olga Burkett, Thomaston, Maine

Stuffed Bluefish

1½ cups bread cubes
¼ cup milk
1 or 2 teaspoons onion soup mix or grated raw

½ teaspoon salt
¼ teaspoon grated lemon rind
1 teaspoon melted margarine

Prepare fish for baking. Mix bread cubes with milk, onion, salt, lemon rind and melted margarine. Stuff the fish and place in a shallow baking pan. Bake in 350 degree oven for 30 to 35 minutes or until done.

Submitted by Mrs. Hazel Hills, Warren, Maine

Fish Salad

1 cup cold flaked fish
1 cup unpeeled apple, diced
1 tablespoon onion, chopped fine

Mayonnaise
Lettuce

Toss fish and apple together lightly. Mix onion with the desired amount of mayonnaise and combine with fish mixture. Serve on crisp lettuce leaves. The red skin of the apple gives color to the salad.

Submitted by Evelyn Dunton, Rockland, Maine

Old-Fashioned Fish Hash

¼ cup bacon fat
1½ cups thinly sliced onions
3 cups peeled, sliced potatoes
1 pound cod fish (or haddock, or white fish) in chunks

⅔ cup milk
Salt and pepper to taste
1 tablespoon minced parsley
2 strips crisply fried bacon

Melt fat in a skillet, add onions and saute over medium heat for a couple of minutes.

Add potatoes, cover skillet, lower heat and cook for 20 minutes, stirring often.

Uncover, add fish, milk, salt and pepper. Cook over low heat, stirring occasionally, until potatoes are lightly browned and milk has been absorbed, 20 to 30 minutes.

Taste for seasoning. Sprinkle with parsley and crumpled crisp bacon and serve.

Submitted by Irene M. Petzolt, Long Island, New York

Codfish Loaf

1 pound codfish (salmon or tuna can be used)
2 cups cooked macaroni
1 cup peas (or carrots)

2 eggs, beaten
1 cup milk
Salt, pepper
1 teaspoon prepared mustard

Mix all together, spoon into a buttered casserole. Top with buttered bread crumbs. Bake at 350 degrees 35 to 45 minutes. Serve with cream sauce or tartar sauce.

Submitted by Ruth A. Savage, Palmyra, Maine

Cod Pie

Leftover cold codfish
12 oysters

Melted butter
Mashed potatoes

Flake the fish from the bones and carefully take away all of the skin. Lay fish in a deep pie dish with the oysters and pour over it the melted butter. Cover with mashed potatoes. Bake for half an hour and send to the table a nice brown color.

Submitted by L. G. Tennies, Westport Island, Wiscasset, Maine

Fish Pie

Often served for lunch in England; cod is often used there as it is cheaper, but I prefer the haddock here in Maine.

3 cups mashed potato
6 to 8 tablespoons milk
2 cups boiled, steamed or canned fish

1 cup parsley sauce or cheese sauce
Margarine or butter for top
Salt and pepper to season

Mash the potato and milk until creamy, season. Line a pie dish with ⅓ of the potato. Flake the fish and mix with the sauce. Season well. Pour into the dish and cover with the rest of the potato. Rough up the top well with a fork so it will look pretty when browned. Bake at 400 degrees until brown on top and heated through, 20 to 30 minutes.

I like parsley sauce and make extra to serve with the pie.
Submitted by Ivy Dodd, Thomaston, Maine

Crisp Oven Fried Fish

1½ pounds fish (cusk, hake or haddock)
3 cups cereal flakes

1 tablespoon salt
1 cup milk
2 tablespoons melted butter

Cut fish into serving pieces, allowing ¼ pound per person. Roll cereal flakes into fine crumbs. Add salt to the milk. Dip fish in milk, then in crumbs, arrange on a well-buttered baking sheet. Dribble melted butter over top of fish. Bake at 500 degrees (this is correct) for 15 to 20 minutes.
Submitted by Marjorie Standish, Gardiner, Maine

Baked Cusk

1½ pounds cusk fillets
Salt, pepper

Butter
½ cup water

Place fillets in a square baking pan. Put salt, pepper and dots of butter on the fish. Add ½ cup of water to the pan and bake until golden brown at 325 degrees for about 30 minutes. Served with baked potatoes and pickled beets, this makes a tasty and colorful dish.

Submitted by Mrs. Lloyd E. Pinkham, Five Islands, Maine

Sweet And Sour Fish

2 pounds flounder fillets
1 can mandarin oranges
  (11 oz. can)
½ cup commercial sweet
  and sour sauce

1 tablespoon cornstarch
1 small onion, sliced in very
  thin rings

Put fillets in a foil-lined baking pan. Drain oranges, mix the juice with cornstarch in a small pan and cook, stirring constantly, over medium heat until mixture thickens. Remove from heat and stir in sweet and sour sauce. Put oranges and thin slices of onion in the baking pan with the fish. Pour sauce over all. Bake in a 350 degree oven for 20 to 30 minutes, or until fish flakes easily when tested. Makes 6 to 8 servings.

Submitted by Mrs. Evelyn Wishart, Sanford, Maine

Breaded Flounder Fillets

1 pound fresh or frozen
  flounder
Juice of 1 lemon
½ cup fine dry bread crumbs

¼ teaspoon paprika
Salt and pepper
1 egg, beaten
¼ cup butter or margarine

Rinse fish under cold water. Put on a paper towel and sprinkle both sides with lemon juice, then lightly with pepper and salt. Mix bread crumbs and paprika. Dip fish in the beaten egg, then in crumbs, coating well. Brown butter lightly in skillet and saute fish over medium heat until it is lightly brown on both sides and flakes easily.

Submitted by Carrie Smalley, Thomaston, Maine

Pan Fried Flounder

5 slices salt pork
Flounder fillets

Cornmeal
Pepper

Fry out the salt pork in fry pan. When pork is brown on both sides, remove from pan. Roll fillets in cornmeal and fry in pork fat on both sides until a golden brown (a little pepper adds flavor).

Serve with a big dish of greens and potatoes.

My father died in 1934 at age 86. He loved what he called "down to earth cooking."

Submitted by Mrs. Dorothy Robbins, Ellsworth, Maine

Baked Fish With Herbed Mayonnaise

2 pounds filets (flounder
   or sole)
3 tablespoons mayonnaise
1/8 teaspoon thyme
1/8 teaspoon onion powder
1/8 teaspoon marjoram

Pinch of tarragon
Pinch of rosemary
1 pimento, chopped
1/3 cup dry vermouth
Salt and pepper to taste

After removing any bones in filets, wash, pat dry, and place filets in greased baking dish (11½ x 7½ x 1¾). (Filets will overlap.) Thoroughly mix next seven ingredients. Spread mayonnaise mixture on top of filets. Pour vermouth over the fish. Bake uncovered at 350 degrees for 30 minutes. Serves 4 to 6.

Submitted by Brewster D. Doggett, Wiscasset, Maine

My Own Fishburgers

1 pound frozen fish fillets
   (cod, haddock or flounder)
Evaporated or rich milk

Commercial clam fry mix
6 hamburger rolls
Tartar sauce

Defrost fish, cut into pieces to fit hamburger roll. Dip each piece in evaporated milk, then into clam fry mix. For a super rich crust, repeat the process so coating will be quite thick. Fry in oil until golden brown on each side. Remove and drain. Then place each piece on a toasted hamburger roll and spread with tartar sauce.

Submitted by Mrs. Dolores Reglin, Orrington, Maine

Baked Fish And Cheese

1 pound fillet, flounder or
   haddock
1/3 cup mayonnaise

1/4 cup Parmesan cheese
2 tablespoons finely ground
   bread crumbs

Brush fillet with mayonnaise. Mix crumbs with the cheese. Roll fish in the crumb mixture and place in a baking dish. Sprinkle the rest of the crumbs on top. Bake at 375 degrees about 30 minutes or until fish is lightly browned.

Submitted by Mrs. Bertha Swift, Lewiston, Maine

Seafood Au Gratin

You can use sole, haddock, flounder, crabmeat or any combination or any one fish.

2 to 3 pounds fish
¼ cup butter
2 cups milk
¼ cup flour
½ teaspoon salt

Dash pepper
1 teaspoon Worcestershire sauce
2 cups shredded sharp cheese
½ cup dry bread crumbs

Melt butter in a saucepan over low heat and blend in the flour; add milk. Cook and stir until thickened. Add salt, pepper, Worcestershire sauce and shredded cheese. Heat until cheese is melted.

Arrange the seafood in the bottom of a shallow baking dish. Pour sauce over the fish and sprinkle with bread crumbs. Bake at 350 degrees for 30 to 35 minutes. Serves 6 to 8.

This is a favorite of my children who like cheesey dishes and a husband who goes fishing for a living.

Submitted by Martha Salminen Tinker, Derry, New Hampshire

Fish Turbot

1 pound haddock or flounder fillet
1 pound shrimp, deveined
1 pound scallops, quartered
½ cup butter
½ cup flour

4 cups hot milk
Salt, pepper, paprika
Butter
(A dash of yellow coloring if wanted)
⅓ cup white cooking sherry

Poach haddock, shrimp and scallops in a small amount of water and drain. Layer in a shallow baking dish. Cover with sauce made as follows.

Cream together butter and flour. Add slowly, beating constantly, the 4 cups of hot milk. Add salt, pepper, color. Cook until thick. Stir in the sherry.

Cover fish with the sauce and dot with butter, sprinkle with paprika and bake at 400 degrees until bubbly.

This turbot was a special for groups at "The House of 1800" buffets. Or served with tossed green salad and the big hard rolls it is perfect for company suppers.

Submitted by Inga J. Chase, Camden, Maine

Old-Fashioned Fish Chowder

1½ pounds fish sticks or
   haddock
1 onion, chopped
4 tablespoons margarine
4 potatoes, peeled and diced

1 can evaporated milk
1 pint milk
Salt and pepper to taste
3 tablespoons butter

Saute onion in the margarine. Add diced potatoes and just cover with water, boil about 20 minutes. Add fish and again cover with water and cook another 20 minutes. Add evaporated milk and the regular milk, bring to simmer. Add salt, pepper and butter. (Pork scraps to saute onion with if preferred instead of margarine.) Serves about 10.

Submitted by Margaret Woodhead, Lewiston, Maine

Fish Chowder

2 pounds haddock (or cod)
1 quart water
¼ pound salt pork
1 small onion, sliced

3 potatoes, sliced
2 teaspoons salt
White pepper to taste
1 quart milk

Cut the fish in small pieces. Put the bones and any trimmings to boil in the water. Dice the pork and cook in heavy pan at low temperature. Cook sliced onion in the pork fat. Add sliced potatoes and the water in which the fish bones were cooked, strained. Add fish and seasonings and cook until fish is done. Add milk and serve with crackers. Pilot biscuits are good.

Submitted by Evelyn Dunton, Rockland, Maine

Maine Fish Chowder

2 pounds haddock
¼ pound salt pork
1 medium onion, chopped
3 cups sliced or diced potatoes

1 quart milk, heated
Salt and pepper to taste
4 ounces butter

Boil the haddock for 15 minutes, remove the bones. Pan fry the salt pork and onions together. Discard the pork. In a large pot boil the potatoes, then add the onions, fish, hot milk, butter and seasonings.

Submitted by Elsie Swanson, Ellsworth, Maine

Easy Fish Chowder

1 small cod
1 halibut nape
8 small potatoes
2 small onions

1 teaspoon salt
¼ pound margarine
2 cups milk

Wash and clean fish, put into uncovered pot with water and boil for 10 minutes. Cool. Pour water into a bowl. Remove fish from the skin and bones. Peel and slice the potatoes and onions. Cook in water until tender. Pour off the water, add fish water and salt, and bring to a boil, add margarine and pieces of fish. When ready to serve, add the milk.

Any fresh fish may be used instead of the cod or halibut.

Submitted by Mabel Batty, South Thomaston, Maine

Seafood Stew

This is a stew that is served at the "Every Member Canvass" meeting at our church. This recipe makes 40 to 50 servings, allowing for seconds and using pint bowls. Depending on the availability and price, other fish may be substituted. We use hake and cusk.

4½ gallons milk
1½ quarts of cream
2½ quarts half and half
9 pounds of haddock, hake or cusk or mixture
2 quarts of liquid in which fish is cooked

2 cans minced clams
1 pound butter
1 gallon oysters
2 pounds frozen Maine shrimp
6 tablespoons or more of salt
½ teaspoon cayenne papper
½ teaspoon pepper

Two large double boilers (25 quarts each) are suggested, the ingredients being divided equally between each.

Cook the fish the day before. Cook until it flakes, pick over and remove any bones. Save the liquid. Refrigerate fish and liquid.

Heat the milk with cream, half and half, and the fish liquid.

Pick over oysters to remove any pieces of shell. Melt butter in a kettle, add the oysters, cover and cook slowly until oysters curl. Then add the oysters to the double boilers. Add the cooked fish, clams and seasonings.

During the last half-hour, cut the frozen shrimp and add to the stew. Taste for further seasoning. Serve in hot bowls. With the stew serve crackers, dill pickles, apple pie and cheese with tea and coffee.

Submitted by Mildred Brown Schrumpf, Orono, Maine

20-Minute Fish Dinner

1 small onion
Green pepper
Pimento
Butter to saute
1 can cream of mushroom
  soup

1 can mushrooms
½ can of milk
Salt and pepper
Haddock, cusk or other
  favorite fish

Saute onion, a little green pepper and pimento in butter. Add the soup, mushrooms, milk, salt and pepper. Add the fish cut in bite size pieces. Heat on top of the stove. Serve with chow mein noodles or rice. Serves 6 to 8.

Submitted by Louise Miller, Cushing, Maine

Fish Pudding

¾ cup butter
6 tablespoons flour
2 teaspoons salt
Pepper
2 cups hot milk

1½ pounds raw fish
6 eggs, separated
Melted butter, Hollandaise
  sauce or dill sauce

Make a heavy cream sauce with the ¾ cup butter blended with flour, salt and pepper. Add the 2 cups of hot milk. Cook until thickened. Grind fine the raw fish, beat egg yolks until thick and add to the white sauce with the ground fish. Beat egg whites until stiff and fold carefully into the cream sauce mixture. Pour into a casserole or baking dish and bake in a water bath at 350 degrees for 1 hour.

Dill Sauce

1 cup sour cream
1 cup mayonnaise

1 tablespoon dill weed
1 teaspoon lemon juice

This recipe is really a souffle and should be served right from the oven. When Mr. Spear was a cook at Sebasco Lodge this recipe became a favorite. At the end of the season they had a "house party" when most meals were served buffet style for a small crowd.

Submitted by Mrs. Lloyd Spear, Rockland, Maine

Fish Pudding

2 pounds fish fillets (haddock
   or cod)
2 teaspoons salt
½ teaspoon pepper

Dash nutmeg
1½ tablespoons cornstarch
2 tablespoons water
1 cup cream

Clean fish and wipe with a clean damp cloth. Force fish through the medium blade of food chopper. Mix in salt, pepper and nutmeg; blend cornstarch with the water to form a smooth paste. Add gradually and stirring in the cup of cream, blend with the fish mixture. Turn into a buttered casserole. Bake in a boiling water bath at 350 degrees for 40 to 50 minutes or until a silver knife comes out clean when inserted halfway between center and edge of casserole. Serve with mushroom sauce.

Mushroom Sauce

Clean and slice ½ cup mushrooms. Heat 1 tablespoon butter in a skillet, add mushrooms and cook until lightly browned and tender. Mix into 1½ cups cooked white sauce.

Submitted by Edith Holmstrom, St. George, Maine

Erdine's Fish Pie

2 cups flaked fish
   (haddock, pollock, etc.)
2 tablespoons butter or
   margarine
2 tablespoons flour
1 cup milk or milk and
   fish water
1 teaspoon salt

1 cup cooked peas (canned
   or frozen)
1 tablespoon grated onion
1 tablespoon chopped green
   pepper
2 cups mashed potato,
   seasoned

Steam or cook the fish in water until it flakes. Prepare a white sauce with butter, flour, milk and ½ teaspoon salt. (Part of the white sauce liquid may be the water from the cooked fish.) To the white sauce add peas, grated onion, green pepper and ½ teaspoon salt. Place the cooked fish in a buttered casserole; pour the sauce over it. Top with well-seasoned mashed potato. (To freshly cooked and mashed potato, add 1 tablespoon butter, ½ cup milk and salt and pepper to taste.) Bake in a hot oven 400 degrees for 12 minutes or until hot and bubbly.

Submitted by Mrs. Richard Dolloff, Orono, Maine

Fish Fillets Rol-Polies

4 fresh fish fillets
4 squares of heavy duty foil
1 cup packaged bread stuffing
1 cup coarse cracker crumbs
4 tablespoons chopped parsley
¼ cup minced onion

¼ cup minced celery
¼ teaspoon salt
Dash pepper
1 tablespoon lemon juice
4 tablespoons melted butter
Boiling water

Combine the stuffing and crumbs with parsley, onion, celery, salt and pepper, adding just enough boiling water to moisten the stuffing. Place each fillet on a square of foil. Spoon dressing into the center of each and roll, tie with a soft string. Brush the rolled fillet with melted butter and sprinkle with lemon juice. Fold foil around the fillet, bring opposite ends up over each roll and overlap 1-inch or more. Turn up opened ends. Place in a shallow pan and bake at 400 degrees for 30 to 40 minutes.

To serve: Slip opened foil packages on to a platter and serve with sauce made as follows:

2 tablespoons butter
1 cup milk
Dash pepper
¼ cup grated cheese

1½ tablespoons flour
½ teaspoon salt
Dash paprika
2 tablespoons lemon juice

Make a sauce with the butter, flour, milk, salt, pepper and paprika. Add grated cheese and lemon juice at the end of cooking.
Submitted by Nancy J. Walter, Hillcrest Heights, Maryland
Formerly of Waldoboro, Maine

Creamed Fish

2 cups cold cooked fish
½ teaspoon salt
1 cup medium white sauce

Dash of nutmeg
Yolk of 1 egg

Add fish to the white sauce and heat thoroughly. Beat egg yolk with salt and nutmeg and add to the sauce just before serving. Heat to the boiling point and serve hot on toast or cornmeal toast.
Submitted by Athelene Hilt, Union, Maine

ERDINE'S FISH PIE combines foods from inland and the shore.
(Recipe on Page 78)

Maine Festival Seafood Pie

1 pound ocean perch or
haddock fillets
(fresh or frozen)
½ cup chopped onion
¼ cup margarine or cooking
oil
¼ cup flour
1 teaspoon salt
Dash pepper
1¼ cups milk

2 tablespoons lemon juice
1 teaspoon Worcestershire
sauce
1 cup fresh or thawed frozen
peas
2 tablespoons chopped
pimento
1 package of pie crust mix
1 teaspoon celery salt
½ teaspoon paprika

Select white-meated fish fillets. Thaw if using frozen fillets. Cut into 1-inch pieces. Saute onion in margarine or cooking oil until tender, but not brown. Stir in the flour, salt and pepper. Add milk gradually; cook, stirring constantly until thickened. Stir in lemon juice and Worcestershire sauce. Fold in the fish pieces, peas and pimento. Set aside and prepare pastry. Mix the pie crust mix as for making a pie, adding salt and paprika. Roll half of the pastry on lightly floured board to ⅛ inch in thickness. Fit into a 9-inch pie plate. Pour filling into lined pie plate. Roll the rest of the pastry and cut several vents to allow for steam to escape. Cover top of pie. Trim and flute the edges. Bake in a 350 degree oven for 30 minutes or until crust is browned and filling is bubbling. Let stand 10 to 15 minutes before cutting into wedges.

Submitted by Mrs. Donald Coffin, Thomaston, Maine

Smothered Fish

1½ pounds fish fillet
1 thinly sliced onion
2 tablespoons butter or
margarine

2 tablespoons flour
Salt, pepper, milk

Generously butter a baking dish. Place sliced onion in the dish in an even layer. Lay the fish over the onions. Sprinkle the flour over the fish, then salt and pepper. Dot with butter. Add milk to about ¼ inch in depth. Bake in a 350 degree oven until fish flakes easily when tested with a fork, about 35 minutes.

Submitted by Mildred Brown Schrumpf, Orono, Maine

Stuffed Haddock
(With Cucumber Stuffing)

1 whole haddock
2 slices bacon
1 small onion
½ cup mushrooms
2 cups pared cucumber, chopped
1 cup soft bread crumbs

¼ teaspoon salt
⅛ teaspoon pepper
2 tablespoons melted butter
2 eggs, beaten
1 lemon, sliced

Chop the bacon, onion and mushrooms and mix well; add cucumber, bread crumbs, salt, pepper and melted butter. Mix well and stir in the eggs. Stuff the cleaned fish and lace the opening together with skewers or wooden picks and thread or string. Place the fish in a greased baking pan and bake in a hot oven 400 degrees for 40 minutes or until the fish flakes easily when it is tested with a fork. A few gashes cut in the skin on each side, before baking, will help keep the fish in shape as it bakes. If the fish is lean, baste with a mixture of melted butter and water during the cooking. Garnish the baked fish with lemon to serve. Other whole fish may be used such as bass or Coho salmon. Fish fillets or halibut steaks also may be used with this stuffing.

Submitted by Mrs. Eldred Hough, Orono, Maine

Fish Souffle

½ cup mayonnaise
4 tablespoons flour
¼ teaspoon salt
Dash pepper
4 tablespoons milk
1 to 1½ cups fish (canned
  or cooked fresh fish, flaked)

2 tablespoons chopped parsley
¼ teaspoon grated onion
1 teaspoon lemon juice
4 egg whites

Mix mayonnaise, flour, salt and pepper, add milk slowly. Stir in fish, parsley, onion, and lemon juice. Beat the egg whites until stiff. Gently fold into the mayonnaise mixture until thoroughly blended. Pour into a greased 7-inch casserole and bake in a 325 degree oven 40 to 45 minutes. Serve at once. Serves 4.

Submitted by Mrs. Flora Smith, Tenants Harbor, Maine

Haddock Rabbit

½ pint cream
Flour
2 cups chopped cheese

1 teaspoon dry mustard
Salt and pepper to taste
Haddock fillet

Make a cream sauce with the cream, a little flour, cheese, mustard, salt and pepper. Put the haddock fillet on a buttered platter, spread sauce over and put in a very hot oven. It should brown in 10 to 15 minutes. Serve with baked potatoes.

Submitted by Mrs. Leland Foster, Wiscasset, Maine

Haddock Rarebit

2 pounds haddock, cut and
   boned
½ cup flour
1 teaspoon dry mustard

Salt to taste
¼ pound margarine
1 cup milk
½ pound American cheese

Make white sauce of flour, mustard, salt, margarine and milk. When thickened, add cheese cut in small pieces. Heat until cheese is melted. Place alternate layers of raw fish and sauce in a greased casserole. Bake 1 hour or until fish is thoroughly cooked.

Submitted by Dorothy Libby, Thomaston, Maine

Fish Rabbit

1 pound haddock fillet
1 tablespoon butter or
   margarine
¼ pound shredded Cheddar
   cheese (about 1 cup)

⅓ cup flour
1 teaspoon salt
1 teaspoon dry mustard
1 cup milk

Place fish fillet in a greased baking dish; spread with the butter. Cover with shredded cheese. In a bowl combine flour, salt, mustard and milk. Mix well and pour over the fish. Bake in a moderate oven 350 degrees for about 1 hour.

Submitted by Mrs. Carl Dow, Winthrop, Maine

Haddock-Shrimp Bake

2 pounds fresh or frozen
  haddock or sole fillets
1 can frozen condensed cream
  of shrimp soup, thawed
¼ cup butter or margarine,
  melted
½ teaspoon grated onion
½ teaspoon Worcestershire
sauce
¼ teaspoon garlic salt
1¼ cups crushed rich round
  crackers (30 crackers)

Slightly thaw frozen fillets. Place fillets in a 13x9x2 inch baking dish. Spread with soup. Bake in a 375 degree oven for 20 minutes. Combine melted butter with seasonings and cracker crumbs. Sprinkle over the fish and bake 10 minutes longer. Makes 6 to 8 servings.
Submitted by Mrs. A. Gertrude Merrill, Rockland, Maine

Haddock Casserole

1½ pounds haddock, cut in
  pieces
1 teaspoon butter
1 teaspoon flour
1 cup canned milk
1 cup cheese, cut up
½ cup tomato soup
Pinch of soda
Salt and pepper to taste
Chopped onion to taste
½ teaspoon dry mustard
Bread crumbs

Mix together the butter, flour, milk, cheese and tomato soup. Also mix together soda, salt, pepper, onion and mustard. Combine these two mixtures with the fish and put into a greased casserole, cover top with bread crumbs. Bake at 350 degrees for 30 minutes.
Submitted by Barbara Moody, Union, Maine

Haddock Casserole

1 pound haddock
1 can cream of shrimp soup
Cheese crackers, crushed
Butter

Put haddock in buttered casserole, cover with the soup. Put crushed crackers on top and dot with plenty of butter. Bake 20 minutes or until fish flakes at 350 degrees. Very nice and easy, too.
Submitted by Gladys Philbrick, Rockland, Maine

Haddock Casserole

2 cups white sauce
½ package of mild cheese
2 hard-cooked eggs
2 cups cooked haddock
(about 1 pound)

2 tablespoons green pepper,
chopped (optional)
Buttered bread crumbs

Dice cheese and egg, flake the haddock, and add to the white sauce. Put in a casserole, top with buttered crumbs. Brown in a 350 degree oven. Delicious served with green peas, sweet potatoes, watermelon pickles and hot rolls.

Submitted by Florence Withee, Newport, Maine

Haddock Casserole

2 pounds haddock fillet
½ cup flour
1 teaspoon dry mustard
1 teaspoon salt

2 tablespoons butter
1½ cups milk
¼ pound American cheese
Paprika

Make sauce of flour, mustard, salt, butter and milk. Cook until thickened, then add the cheese (cut in small pieces). Continue to cook until cheese is melted. Place alternate layers of fish and sauce in a buttered casserole, ending with sauce. Sprinkle paprika on top. Bake in a 350 degree oven until fish is thoroughly cooked.

Submitted by Edna H. Monteith, Rockland, Maine

Haddock Casserole

1 pound fresh haddock
1 can cream of shrimp soup

½ cup milk
Salt and pepper

Place haddock in a greased casserole. Mix well the milk and soup. Add salt and pepper to taste. Pour milk-soup mixture over haddock in casserole and bake at 350 degrees for 30 to 40 minutes.

Submitted by Norma Brown, Newport, Maine

Haddock Casserole

1½ pounds fresh or frozen
   haddock fillets
1 cup fine-cut cheese

1 cup bread crumbs, also fine
1 can mushroom soup
1 can evaporated milk

Place fillets in shallow baking pan, mix other ingredients, and turn them over fish, topping with bread crumbs. Bake in 350 degree oven for 45 minutes; serves six. (Cod or hake may be substituted for haddock if desired.)
Submitted by Mrs. Chester Stone, Owls Head, Maine

Haddock And Scallop Casserole

½ pound haddock fillets
½ pound scallops
1 small can frozen shrimp
   soup (thawed)

Buttered coarse bread crumbs

Cut scallops in half. Cook scallops and haddock for 5 minutes in boiling water. Drain and separate in bite-size pieces. Place in a buttered casserole and pour shrimp soup over the fish. Top with buttered bread crumbs. Bake ½ hour at 350 degrees.
Submitted by Phyllis Copeland, Thomaston, Maine

Leone's Fish Casserole

3 cups soft bread crumbs
   (6 or 7 slices)
1½ pounds haddock fillets
1 medium onion, minced
2 cans cream of mushroom
   soup, undiluted

1 teaspoon salt
1 teaspoon fish herbs
Buttered herbed crumbs

Cut fish fillets in small cubes. In a buttered casserole, layer ½ of the crumbs, onion, fish and 1 can of mushroom soup undiluted and sprinkle with salt and fish herbs. Repeat the layers. Sprinkle with buttered herbed crumbs. (You may make your own mixture of fish herbs by mixing dried dill, thyme, basil and parsley.) Herbed crumbs are the stuffing mixture found in your market. Bake in a moderate oven (350 degrees) for 1¼ hours.
Submitted by Mrs. Albert D. Nutting, Oxford, Maine

Fish Casserole

½ cup butter
1 medium onion, chopped
½ cup flour
1 teaspoon salt
Few grains of pepper

3 cups milk
2 pounds fish fillets
Cheese slices
3 or 4 medium raw potatoes

Melt butter in a saucepan over low heat. Saute chopped onion until transparent. Blend in flour, salt and pepper. Add gradually the 3 cups of milk. Bring to a boil and set aside. Grease a casserole and prepare fillets. Lay half in the casserole and top with cheese slices. Pour over half of the sauce, add rest of the fish and top with slices of raw potatoes. Top with rest of the sauce. Bake in a 350 degree oven for 30 to 40 minutes.

Submitted by Lois Whitcomb, Morrill, Maine

Fish Casserole

¼ cup flour
1 teaspoon dry mustard
Salt, pepper to taste
1 cup milk, heated

4 tablespoons butter
¼ pound cheese
2 pounds fish

Combine flour, mustard, salt and pepper. Mix with the hot milk, add butter and cheese. Stir until cheese melts. Place fish in buttered casserole and pour the sauce mixture over top. Bake in 350 degree oven until fish tests done.

Submitted by Nellie Ifemey, Thomaston, Maine

Fish Casserole

Haddock
Parmesan cheese
Salt and pepper

1 can cream of mushroom
soup

Place layers of haddock in a greased casserole dish. Sprinkle generously with Parmesan cheese. Add salt and pepper, another layer of fish, then pour the mushroom soup over all. Put some cheese on top. Bake 1 hour at 350 degrees.

Submitted by Martha Wilson, Thomaston, Maine

Fish Casserole

2 cups haddock fillets, flaked
1 cup medium sharp cheese, shredded
1 can cream of mushroom soup
½ cup milk
1 small jar mushrooms
1 jar pimentos
1½ cups cooked macaroni or noodles
Crumbled cheese crackers for top

Mix all together and pour into a greased casserole. Sprinkle crumbled crackers over the top. Bake at 350 degrees for 40 minutes.

Submitted by Minerva Small, Rockland, Maine

Fish Casserole

1½ pounds fish
3 tablespoons butter
1 large carrot, grated
3 pieces celery, chopped
½ green pepper, chopped
1 medium onion, chopped
2 tablespoons flour
½ cup milk
1 can mushroom soup
¾ cup grated cheese
Salt and pepper to taste
4 slices bread, cubed

Melt butter, add carrot, celery, pepper and onion and cook slowly about 5 minutes. Mix in flour, add milk and cook until thickened.

Add soup and when hot, add the cheese and cook until cheese is melted.

Put ½ of fish in a buttered casserole, a little salt and pepper, ½ of the sauce and ½ of the cubed bread. Repeat process ending with bread cubes. Bake 350 degrees over 1 hour.

Submitted by Nancy Clark, Newport, Maine

Fish Casserole

1 pound haddock
1 pound scallops
2 cans cream of shrimp soup
Bread crumbs
Butter

Cook haddock and scallops for 10 minutes, flake in a casserole. Add the shrimp soup, thawed. Top with crumbs and butter. Bake at 350 degrees for ½ hour or until bubbly.

Submitted by Lois Burr, Old Town, Maine

Seafood Casserole

1 pound haddock, cooked
1 pound scallops, cooked
1 pound lobster, cooked
1 can mushroom soup

½ can milk
Butter
1 cup buttered crumbs

Place pieces of fish in a buttered casserole, cover with soup and milk, dot with butter. Put buttered crumbs over top. Bake in 325 degree oven 30 minutes.

Submitted by Claribel Andrews, Tenants Harbor, Maine

Fish-Stix Casserole

1 package fish stix
1 can tomato sauce (8 oz.)
1 teaspoon onion
½ teaspoon salt

Pepper to taste
Dash of basil and oregano
1 cup Mozarella cheese

Place fish in baking dish. Combine next six ingredients, pour over fish and top with cheese. Bake for 20 minutes in a 300 degree oven or until cheese melts.

Submitted by Rae Kontio, Augusta, Maine

Creamed Fish Casserole

4 tablespoons margarine
¼ cup diced green papper
6 tablespoons flour
1¼ teaspoons salt
¼ teaspoon pepper
2½ cups milk

2 cups cooked or canned fish
¼ cup diced pimento
1⅓ cups crispy crackers,
    crushed
Butter

Melt shortening over low heat; add green pepper and saute 5 minutes. Blend in flour, salt and pepper. Remove from heat and gradually stir in milk. Return to heat and cook, stirring constantly, until thick and smooth. Add fish, pimento and one cup of the cracker crumbs; mix well. Turn into a greased casserole and top with remaining cracker crumbs. Dot with butter. Bake in a 350 degree oven 30 to 40 minutes.

Submitted by Evelyn Dunton, Rockland, Maine

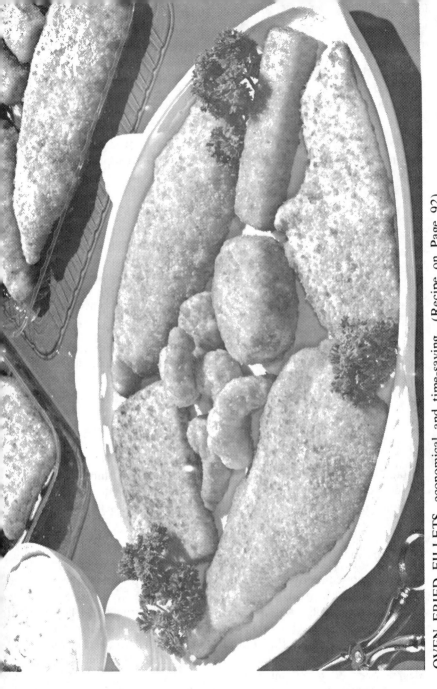

OVEN FRIED FILLETS, economical and time-saving. (Recipe on Page 92)

Creole Style Haddock

2 pounds fish fillets
(fresh or frozen)
3 vegetable bouillon cubes
3 cups boiling water
¾ cup chopped onion
¼ cup chopped celery
2 small cloves garlic,
finely chopped
½ cup melted fat or oil
¼ cup flour
1 can (10½ oz.) tomato puree
1 bay leaf

1 tablespoon Worcestershire
sauce
1½ teaspoons salt
1 teaspoon thyme
½ teaspoon sugar
⅛ teaspoon red pepper
⅛ teaspoon liquid hot pepper
sauce
3 cups hot cooked rice
¼ cup chopped parsley

Cut fish into 2-inch pieces. Dissolve bouillon in boiling water, set aside. Cook onion, celery and garlic in fat until tender in a fry pan. Blend in flour and cook until lightly browned. Add bouillon, tomato puree and seasonings. Simmer uncovered for 30 minutes, stirring occasionally. Add fish, simmer 10-15 minutes longer until fish flakes easily when tested with a fork. Combine rice and parsley. Serve Creole Style Haddock over rice. (Other fish can be used instead of haddock.) Serves 6.

Submitted by Nancy J. Walter, Hillcrest Height, Maryland

Broiled Fish Fillets

1 pound fish fillets (haddock
or sole)
¼ cup lemon juice
2 tablespoons butter
1 tablespoon grated onion

1 tablespoon brown sugar
½ teaspoon dry mustard
¼ teaspoon salt
Pinch of pepper

Arrange fish in a baking pan. Heat lemon juice, butter, onion, sugar, mustard, salt and pepper in a small saucepan until well blended. Pour ⅔ of the sauce over the fish and broil about 4 inches from broiler heat, basting often with remaining sauce. Fish should be browned and flakes nicely. Sprinkle with paprika and serve.

Submitted by Mrs. Bertha Swift, Lewiston, Maine

Oven Fried Fillets

1 pound to 1½ pounds
  haddock fillets
1 egg
1 tablespoon water

Bread or cracker crumbs
½ cup melted butter or
  margarine

Beat egg with water and dip fish in this egg mixture. Roll in crumbs (on wax paper). Place fish in a shallow baking pan. Cover with melted butter or margarine. Bake in a 500 degree oven until brown and flaky about 10 to 12 minutes.

Submitted by Nancy Lamb, Rockland, Maine

Baked Stuffed Fillets

4 or 5 haddock fillets
1 cup bread crumbs
Salt and pepper to taste
1 can minced clams, drained
  (save liquid)

1 small onion, diced
2 tablespoons tomato sauce

If fillets are large, cut them into serving size. Carefully remove all bones. Make stuffing with bread crumbs, salt, pepper, clams, onion and tomato sauce (or clam liquid instead of tomato sauce). Spread this on the fish and roll each piece. Fasten with skewer or pick and place on a greased pan. Bake at 350 degrees for 25 minutes or until fish flakes easily. Clams may be omitted and herbs added to stuffing.

Submitted by Ruth A. Savage, Palmyra, Maine

Baked Fish Fillets
(Hake, Haddock, Cod)

2 pounds fish fillets, cut in
  serving size pieces
2 beaten eggs

Butter

Paprika
1½ cups cracker crumbs or
  cornflakes

Pat fish dry in paper towels and dip the fillets in the beaten eggs, then in cracker crumbs. Place fillets in a greased pan, dot with butter, sprinkle with paprika. Bake at 400 degrees for 20 minutes.

Submitted by Bodine Ames, Vinalhaven, Maine

Baked Haddock Fillet

1 pound haddock
Pepper
1 can cream of shrimp soup

4 slices bread, crumbled
Butter

Cut haddock into serving pieces, put in greased casserole, sprinkle with pepper. Cover with shrimp soup, sprinkle crumbs over top, and dot with butter. Bake 1 hour in 350 degree oven.
Submitted by Martha Wilson, Thomaston, Maine

Haddock With Shrimp Sauce

1½ pounds fillet of haddock
1 can frozen shrimp soup
Seasoning to taste
Parmesan cheese
Place fillets in a baking dish and cover with undiluted soup. Season to taste and sprinkle with Parmesan cheese.
Bake at 350 degrees until soup bubbles and browns slightly.
Submitted by Grace H. Perkins, Bangor, Maine

Stuffed Fish Fillet

4 fish fillets 1½ pounds
  (haddock or flounder)
2 tablespoons chopped onion
¼ cup chopped celery
2 tablespoons butter or
  margarine
2 tablespoons milk (may need
  a bit more)

2 tablespoons chopped green
  pepper
½ teaspoon salt
¼ teaspoon thyme
Dash of pepper
1¼ cups soft bread crumbs
Prepare a cheese sauce or use
  canned Cheddar cheese.

Saute onion, celery and green pepper in butter until tender but not brown. Add to the bread crumbs with salt, thyme and pepper; mix well. Add milk to moisten the bread mixture.

Place half of the fish fillets in a greased baking pan (I use oven-proof glass) and cover with stuffing. Place rest of fillets on top of stuffing. Pour cheese sauce over the fish. Bake at 350 degrees for 30 minutes or until tender. Serve at once. Serves 4 to 6.
Submitted by Mrs. Harlan H. Bragdon, St. George, Maine

Haddock Au Gratin

2½ cups of flaked haddock or any white fish, cooked
3 hard-cooked eggs, coarsely chopped
2 cups white sauce
1 teaspoon lemon juice
½ cup soft bread crumbs
½ cup grated Cheddar cheese
2 tablespoons butter or margarine

Combine haddock and eggs with white sauce and lemon juice. Place all in a buttered casserole dish, cover with the crumbs, cheese and dot with butter. Bake about 25 minutes at 350 degrees until crumbs are nicely browned. For variation I sometimes mix a little poultry seasoning with the bread crumbs.

Submitted by Irma W. Benner, South Harpswell, Maine

Mustard Fish And Chips

1½ pounds frozen fish fillets, thawed
6 tablespoons mayonnaise
1 tablespoon prepared mustard
1 tablespoon instant minced onion
Paprika
1 pound frozen French-fried potatoes

Put fillets in shallow buttered baking dish. Mix next 3 ingredients and spread on fish. Sprinkle with paprika. Arrange potatoes in a shallow pan. Bake fish and potatoes in extremely hot oven (500 degrees) 15 to 20 minutes.

Submitted by Elsie Swanson, Ellsworth, Maine

Fish-in-the-Skillet

4 fish steaks
¼ cup flour
1 teaspoon salt
1 egg
2 tablespoons water
½ cup fine dry crumbs
½ cup vegetable shortening

Mix flour and salt together. Beat egg with the water. Dip fish in seasoned flour, then into the egg mixture and finally in crumbs. Heat shortening in a frying pan and fry fish until tender and golden brown on each side, about 20 minutes. Meanwhile, mix up "Hush Puppies" which can be cooked in the frying pan along with the fish.

continued

"Hush Puppies"

2 cups cornmeal
1 tablespoon flour
½ teaspoon soda
1 teaspoon baking powder

1 teaspoon salt
2 tablespoons chopped onion
1 cup buttermilk
1 egg, beaten

Mix dry ingredients together, add onion, buttermilk and egg. Mix well. Drop by spoonfuls into the pan in which fish is being fried. Fry to a golden brown. Drain on absorbent paper. Makes 4 servings.

Submitted by Elsie Swanson, Ellsworth, Maine

Baked Haddock With Crabmeat Stuffing

1 (3 lb.) haddock
1½ cups flaked crabmeat
¼ cup finely chopped celery
¼ cup tart apple, chopped fine
1 tablespoon green pepper, minced
1 tablespoon minced pimento

1 cup soft bread crumbs
1 egg, well beaten
2 tablespoons butter, melted
Parsley
1 lime, sliced

Prepare the haddock for baking. Set aside. Mix together crabmeat, celery, apple, green pepper, pimento, bread crumbs and the well beaten egg. Stuff the fish, place in greased baking dish, brush with melted butter and bake in a 350 degree oven for 1 hour or until tests done. Garnish with parsley and sliced lime.

Submitted by Leland C. Foster, Wiscasset, Maine

Baked Fish With Vegetable Topper

2 cups soft bread crumbs
1 teaspoon salt
2 tablespoons chopped onion
¼ cup shortening, melted

¼ cup hot water
2 1-pound fillets
2 cans condensed vegetable soup

Combine bread crumbs, salt, onion and shortening. Add water and mix well. Spread between the two pieces of fish in a greased baking dish. Cover with the soup. Bake at 350 degrees for 30 minutes.

Submitted by Margaret Jenny, Belgrade, Maine

Baked Haddock With Cheese

1½ pounds haddock fillet
4 tablespoons margarine or
butter
¼ cup flour
½ teaspoon salt

½ teaspoon dry mustard
¼ teaspoon paprika
⅛ teaspoon pepper
2 cups milk
¾ cup grated cheese

Place fillets in a well buttered baking dish. Prepare a cheese sauce by blending margarine and flour with seasonings. Add milk and cook over low heat until the sauce is thick and smooth, stirring constantly. Add cheese and let stand until cheese has melted. Pour sauce over the fish and bake in moderate oven 350 degrees for 30 minutes or until the fish flakes when tested with a fork.

Submitted by Mrs. Dolores Reglin, Orrington, Maine

Baked Haddock Cheddar

Put fresh or thawed frozen fish fillets in greased, shallow baking dish. Sprinkle with salt and pepper. Dot with butter. Shake on bread crumbs to cover. Layer Cheddar cheese on top. Bake in 350 degree oven for approximately 15 minutes.

Submitted by Eleanor C. Linton, Camden, Maine

Baked Fish In Tomato Sauce

2 carrots, sliced
2 large onions, sliced
2 sweet peppers, cut in small pieces
1 can tomato soup

½ cup milk
Salt and pepper to taste
2 pounds haddock fillets

Parboil the vegetables for 10 minutes. Drain, place in the bottom of a buttered baking dish. Mix soup with milk and pour over vegetables. Cut fish in serving size pieces and place on top of casserole, sprinkle with salt and pepper. Bake in a hot oven (375 to 400 degrees) for 30 minutes or until fish flakes easily.

Submitted by Mrs. Thomas J. Johnson, North Edgecomb, Maine

Baked Haddock

1 pound haddock fillets
1 small onion, cut up
1 tablespoon flour
½ teaspoon pepper

½ teaspoon salt
5 crackers, crushed
Milk
Butter, 1 tablespoon

Place fillets in buttered dish, sprinkle onion, flour, pepper, salt and crushed crackers over fish. Cover with milk. Dot with butter. Bake about 1 hour at 400 degrees.

Submitted by Mrs. Elvie Shields, Thomaston, Maine

Baked Haddock

1 pound haddock fillets
(frozen or fresh)
1 can frozen cream of shrimp
soup

2 tablespoons milk
¼ cup buttered bread crumbs
Paprika and parsley

Slowly heat soup and milk in top of double boiler until soup is melted. Stir thoroughly. Arrange fillets on greased dish (if using frozen fillets, thaw) cover with soup and milk mixture and top with buttered crumbs. Bake in hot oven 15-20 minutes until fish is just tender. Sprinkle with paprika and garnish with parsley. Serves 3.

Submitted by Corinne W. Small, Damariscotta, Maine

Baked Haddock

1 (4 lb.) haddock
Grated American cheese
Salt and pepper to taste
Butter
Milk

Split, bone and skin a 4-pound haddock. Put in a greased baking dish. Sprinkle heavily with grated American cheese. Season to taste with salt and pepper, dot with butter and add enough milk to just cover. Bake in moderate oven 350 degrees 45 to 50 minutes until nicely browned. (Mackerel may be baked the same way.)

Submitted by Eva Meservey, Jefferson, Maine

BAKED HADDOCK WITH CHEESE makes a good lunch or supper dish. (Recipe on Page 96)

Baked Haddock

2 pounds haddock
4 tablespoons butter
½ cup flour

1 tablespoon mustard
1 cup milk
¼ pound mild cheese

In the top of a double boiler make a sauce using butter, flour, mustard and milk. Cook over boiling water, stirring constantly until thick. Add the cut-up cheese and cook until cheese is melted, stir occasionally. This will be a very thick sauce.

Place layers of raw haddock in a pan or casserole. Spread thick sauce over the haddock. As the fish cooks, the liquid from the fish makes a sauce of the right consistency and very tasty. Bake at 350 degrees for one hour or until tender.

This is a recipe that the Beaverettes used at Knox County Fish and Game suppers. It was made in big pans, easy to make and delicious.

The ovens where the fish was baked were heated with wood and this gave a good smoked flavor to the fish.

If anyone likes a smoky flavor, smoky cheese can be used.

Submitted by Ruth C. Wiggin, Thomaston, Maine

Poor Man's Lobster

1 pound haddock fillets
1 tablespoon vinegar

Hot melted butter
Paprika

Cover fish with cold water and vinegar and bring to a boil on medium heat, boil for 10 minutes. Drain and serve with hot melted butter and a sprinkling of paprika. Very tasty.

Submitted by Mrs. Bertha Swift, Lewiston, Maine

Poor Man's Lobster

1 pound frozen haddock
2 tablespoons vinegar

2 tablespoons salt
Butter, melted

Place haddock in a covered skillet, cover with cold water, add vinegar. Bring to a boil and simmer for 10 minutes. Pour off water and recover with more cold water, adding the salt. Bring again to a boil and simmer for 10 more minutes. Drain. Serve with melted butter.

Submitted by Marie Graves, Waterville, Maine

Haddock And Sauce

2-pound fish
1 can frozen shrimp soup
1 cup sour cream
3 tablespoons lemon juice

Salt and pepper to taste
Green peppers or onions
(optional)

Make a sauce by combining the soup, sour cream, lemon juice, salt and pepper. Place fish in a buttered baking dish and bake for 25 minutes at 375 degree temperature. Now add the sauce and cook for about 5 minutes more. Slice peppers or onions over top if desired.

Submitted by Mrs. Austin W. Miller, Friendship, Maine

Indian Recipe For Fish

Haddock fillets
Salt, pepper

Sliced tomato
1 green pepper, chopped

Salt and pepper each fillet, place sliced tomato on top, some chopped green pepper. Wrap in foil and bake. Moist and delicious.

Submitted by Nellie Ifemey, Thomaston, Maine

Fish Scallop Or Rarebit

2 pounds haddock fillets
½ cup flour
1 teaspoon dry mustard
Salt to taste

⅛ pound butter or margarine
1 cup milk
½ pound American cheese,
cut up

Mix together the flour, mustard, salt, butter and milk. Heat until thickened then add the cheese, continue to heat. Place fish and cheese sauce in layers in casserole. Bake 1 hour.

Submitted by Leona Starrett, Thomaston, Maine

Scalloped White Fish

2 cups cooked haddock or cod
2 cups diced white potatoes
Scant teaspoon paprika
Scant teaspoon salt
1 tablespoon minced green pepper
1½ cups medium white sauce
1 hard-cooked egg, chopped

1 teaspoon lemon juice
½ cup buttered bread
   crumbs
Parsley flakes

Cook the fish for 10 minutes in water to cover. Drain and cook potatoes in the fish water. Mix potato, salt, pepper and paprika together. Mix flaked fish, chopped egg, and lemon juice together. Butter a 2-quart casserole and add a layer of the potato mixture, then a layer of fish until all are used up. Pour the white sauce over all. Sprinkle with buttered bread crumbs and a dash of parsley flakes. Bake at 350 degrees for 25 minutes.

Submitted by Ivis M. Fowle, Newport, Maine

Scalloped Haddock

1½ pounds haddock (cooked)
4 tablespoons flour
4 tablespoons butter
½ teaspoon mustard

2 cups milk
¾ cup grated cheese
Crumbs

Prepare a white sauce with flour, butter, mustard and milk. Add grated cheese. Flake haddock into a greased baking dish and pour the sauce over it. Top with crumbs and bake 30 minutes in a 350 degree oven. Sauteed onion and/ or green pepper may be added, also hard-cooked eggs.

Submitted by Mrs. Alexander C. Stewart, Waldoboro, Maine

Fish Sandwiches

Leftover fried fish (halibut or
   haddock)

Salt to taste
Tartar sauce

Flake the cold fish and remove any bones. Mix with enough tartar sauce to moisten thoroughly. Salt to taste. Serve on white bread. This makes a very tasty sandwich, especially the halibut.

Submitted by Mrs. Roland P. Nadeau, Bangor, Maine

Summer Haddock

2 haddock fillets
1 onion
1 tomato

1 green pepper
Butter
1 cup milk

Cut fillets in squares and place in a glass baking dish about 1 inch apart. Top each piece with a layer of onion, tomato, green pepper and a dot of butter. Add 1 cup of milk and bake about 20 minutes at 350 degrees. This tastes great and makes an attractive serving.

Submitted by Mrs. Thomas A. Watson, Five Islands, Maine

Peppers Stuffed With Halibut

4 large peppers (green sweet)
1 tablespoon butter
½ medium onion, minced
½ cup soft bread crumbs
1 cup cooked flaked halibut
½ cup milk

½ teaspoon salt
1 teaspoon lemon juice
1 egg, slightly beaten
¼ cup buttered crumbs
¼ cup grated cheese

Cut top slice from peppers and remove seeds. Boil 3 minutes and drain. Melt butter in skillet and cook the minced onion over low heat. Stir in ½ cup soft bread crumbs, the halibut, milk, salt and lemon juice. Stir in the slightly beaten egg. Fill pepper shells and sprinkle with top with buttered crumbs and grated cheese. Bake in a 350 degree oven until a delicate brown.

Submitted by Leland C. Foster, Wiscasset, Maine

Fish Turbot

2 pounds halibut
1 quart milk
1 onion, cut fine
2 tablespoons flour

½ cup butter
2 eggs, beaten
Bread crumbs

Cook fish until done, by boiling or steaming. Boil milk with onion gently for ½ hour, then strain. Cream flour with butter and beat in the eggs. Add this mixture to the milk and cook until well thickened. When cold, add the fish picked fine. Alternate layers of fish and cream sauce, with bread crumbs on top (in a well-greased baking dish). Bake at 350 degrees for 20 minutes.

Submitted by Elizabeth H. French, Auburn, Maine

Halibut Baked In Cheese Sauce

2 halibut steaks (1 pound each)
2 tablespoons butter
2 tablespoons lemon juice
¼ cup butter
¼ cup flour
1 teaspoon salt
Dash pepper

2 cups milk
1 cup shredded Cheddar cheese
3 tablespoons grated Parmesan cheese
2 hard-cooked eggs, sieved

Broil halibut with 2 tablespoons butter, 15 or 20 minutes or until fish flakes. Place fish in a 2-quart baking dish. Sprinkle with lemon juice. In a saucepan melt the ¼ cup of butter, add flour, salt and pepper. Blend well, remove from heat and gradually stir in the milk. Cook over medium heat while stirring until thickened. Remove from heat and stir in the cup of grated cheese. Pour sauce over the fish, sprinkle on cheese and bake at 350 degrees for 20 minutes. Sprinkle on the sieved egg.

Submitted by Mrs. Priscilla Woodward, Warren, Maine

Quick Baked Fish

2 large halibut or haddock steaks, ½ inch thick
2 teaspoons salt
½ cup milk
1½ cups crushed corn flakes
2 tablespoons melted butter or margarine
1 tablespoon butter, melted
1 tablespoon flour

½ cup milk
⅓ cup mayonnaise
1 teaspoon vinegar
2 tablespoons chopped olives
2 tablespoons chopped dill pickle
1 teaspoon onion juice

Dip fish steaks into the salted milk. Coat thoroughly with crushed corn flakes. Place on a greased baking sheet; drizzle with butter. Bake in a hot oven 500 degrees for 10 minutes (or until flakes easily). Make a **Hot Tartar Sauce** as follows: melt the 1 tablespoon butter, and blend in 1 tablespoon flour. Gradually stir in ½ cup of milk and cook over low heat until smooth and thick, stirring constantly. Stir in mayonnaise, vinegar, olives, dill pickles and onion juice. Heat thoroughly. Makes ¾ cup. This recipe makes 4 servings.

Submitted by Mrs. A. Gertrude Merrill, Rockland, Maine

Helen's Halibut Loaf

1 pound raw halibut, chopped
   fine
Equal amount of bread crumbs
1 cup cream

1 teaspoon butter
1½ teaspoons celery salt
4 egg whites, stiffly beaten

Cook to a smooth paste the crumbs and the cream. Add to the chopped fish with butter and celery salt. Fold in stiffly beaten egg whites. Pour into baking dish. Put baking dish in a pan of hot water. Bake in a 350 degree oven until done. Serve with lobster sauce or cheese sauce.

Submitted by Mrs. Bernard Deering, Orono, Maine

Baked Halibut With Tomato Sauce

Halibut
Salt, pepper, and flour for
   dredging
Few slices of salt pork

Few slices of onion
Hot water
Tomato sauce

Put a few slices of salt pork and onions in a baking dish and put the fish on top of this. Put a few slices of pork and onions on top of fish. Pour hot water in the dish to the depth of an inch and bake at 350 degrees until fish is nearly done, about 30 minutes. Then pour the tomato sauce over it and finish cooking or until fish will break away from bones easily.

Submitted by Grace Irvine, Warren, Maine

Baked Halibut Parmesan

Halibut steaks or fillets
Salt, or seasoned salt
Pepper
Paprika

Butter or margarine
½ cup bread crumbs
½ cup Parmesan cheese

Put fresh or thawed frozen halibut steaks or fillets in a greased shallow baking dish. Sprinkle to taste with salt or seasoned salt, pepper and paprika. Dot generously with butter or margarine. Bake in a 325 degree oven for about 15 minutes. Remove fish from oven and spread with a mixture of bread crumbs and cheese. Dot with more butter, and bake 15-20 minutes more.

Submitted by Eleanor C. Linton, Camden, Maine

Easy Fish Dinner

1 pound haddock fillets
½ teaspoon salt
⅛ teaspoon pepper

⅛ teaspoon oregano
½ teaspoon parsley flakes
1 can cream of celery soup

Cut fish in four serving pieces and place in greased baking dish. Sprinkle the fish pieces with salt, pepper, oregano and parsley flakes. Pour on and spread the undiluted celery soup. Bake at 375 degrees about 45 minutes.

Submitted by Mrs. Harry Stewart, Union, Maine

Pan Fried Mackerel

Mackerel
Cornmeal

Salt
Bacon drippings

Clean and wash fish. Divide each fish into two strips lengthwise. Dip strips into salted cornmeal, saute in bacon drippings until crisp and brown. Do both sides. Serve with lemon.

Submitted by Priscilla Woodward, Warren, Maine

Spanish Mackerel

1 mackerel, about 2 pounds
½ cup chopped onion
½ cup chopped green pepper
¼ to ½ stick butter (depending on size of fish)

1 can tomato sauce
Salt and pepper.

Split the fish and lay skin side down. Spread softened butter over fish, salt and pepper. Add chopped onion and green pepper. Pout tomato sauce over all. Bake in a 350 degree oven until done.

Submitted by Nellie Ifemey, Thomaston, Maine

G'ma Young's Spiced Mackerel

Mackerel for canning
1 teaspoon pickling salt
1 teaspoon ground allspice

1 teaspoon sugar
Vinegar to fill jar

Prepare fish as to cook for eating. In the bottom of each sterilized jar put salt, allspice and sugar, and pack full of fish. Fill jar with vinegar (after fish have been packed in). Seal and cook in pressure cooker for 1 hour and 40 minutes at 10 pounds pressure. Store in cool dry place. Serve hot or cold.
Submitted by Mrs. Irving H. Parsons, Stockton Springs, Maine

Soused Mackerel

8 mackerel
1 teaspoon salt
1 teaspoon sugar
1 onion, sliced

6 cloves
1 teaspoon peppercorns
1 bay leaf
1 cup vinegar

Put fish into a casserole after cleaning them, sprinkle with seasonings and pour the vinegar over. Cover and bake in a very slow oven 275 to 300 degrees for at least 1½ hours. Longer cooking improves the flavor and softens the bones so they can be eaten. Refrigerate in the dish to become quite cold and serve with some of the strained liquor as a sauce. Good with potatoes and a salad.

Submitted by Ivy Dodd, Thomaston, Maine

HOW

TO EAT

MAINE LOBSTER . . .

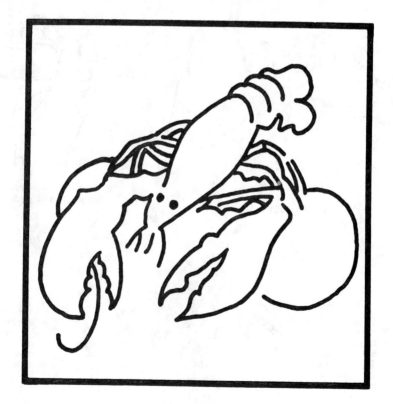

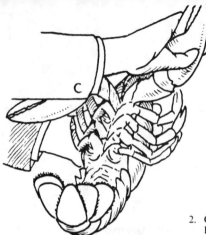

1. Twist off the claws.

2. Crack each claw with a nutcracker, pliers, hammer, rock or what have you.

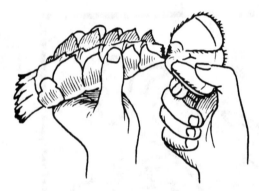

4. Bend back and break the flippers off the tail-piece.

5. Insert a fork where the ▮ broke off and push.

7. Open the remaining part of the body by cracking a p a r t sideways. There is s o m e good meat in this section.

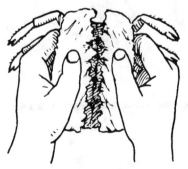

8. The small are excellen ing and m p l a c e d i mouth an meat sucke like sipping with a straw

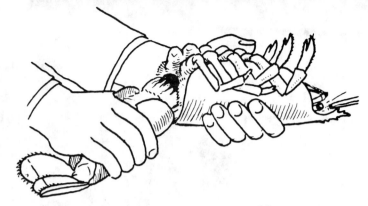

3. Separate the tail-piece from the body by arching the back until it cracks.

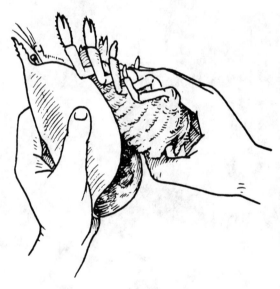

6. Unhinge the back from the body. Don't forget that this contains the "tomalley," or liver of the lobster which turns green when it is cooked and which many persons consider the best eating of all.

Mackerel Maine Style

2 mackerel (about 2 pounds each)
1 large onion, chopped fine
1 large carrot, diced fine
½ green pepper, chopped
¾ cup vinegar
½ teaspoon salt
1 tablespoon chopped parsley
¼ teaspoon thyme, minced
1 bay leaf

Make a sauce with onion, carrot, green pepper, vinegar, salt, parsley, thyme and bay leaf. Cook over low heat about 20 minutes. Prepare mackerel for eating and place in an oblong baking dish. Cover with the sauce (take out the bay leaf). Pre-heat oven to 400 degrees and bake fish 30 to 40 minutes. Serves 4 to 6.
Submitted by Mrs. Gloria Matthews Simmons, Rockland, Maine

Mackerel Baked In Vinegar And Butter

1 mackerel, about 2 pounds
¼ to ½ stick butter (depending on size of fish)
Vinegar to cover fish
Salt and pepper.

Split the fish and lay skin side down. Spread softened butter over fish, add salt and pepper, cover with vinegar and bake in a 350 degree oven until done.
Submitted by Nellie Ifemey, Thomaston, Maine

Broiled Mackerel

Clean 3 good size mackerel. Line a broiler pan with aluminum foil. Lay the mackerel on it, heads opposite tails. Do not cover. Salt and pepper optional. Broil for 10 or 15 minutes until golden brown. These are very good.
Submitted by Mrs. Hazel Firth, Rockland, Maine

Crusty Salmon Steaks

4 salmon steaks (about ¾ inch thick)
2 eggs
1 tablespoon lemon juice
2 tablespoons light cream
½ teaspoon salt
1 cup cracker meal
2 tablespoons butter

Beat together the eggs, lemon juice, cream and salt. Dip steaks in this mixture than roll in the cracker meal. Fry in butter.
Submitted by Dorothy Larrabee, Glen Cove, Maine

Salmon Roll With Egg Sauce

1 cup sifted flour
2 teaspoons baking powder
¼ teaspoon salt
4 tablespoons shortening
1 tablespoon butter
⅓ cup sweet milk
2 eggs
2 cups red salmon (freshly caught, boiled and flaked) or 1 can

Sift together the flour, baking powder and salt. Cut in the shortening with blender or fingers. Stir in the milk and mix well, and turn on floured board. Knead lightly and roll into rectangular shape about ¼ inch thick. Remove the skin and bones from the salmon, mix thoroughly and spread over the dough. Roll up jelly roll fashion and place in a greased 9 x 13 inch greased baking pan. Beat the other egg and brush top of roll with part of it. Combine the remaining part of the egg with the remaining cup of salmon and arrange around the salmon roll. Dot roll with the tablespoon of butter and bake in a moderate oven (375 degrees) until well done, approximately 45 minutes. Be sure it isn't sticky in the center. Serve with the following egg sauce:

Egg Sauce

3 tablespoons oleo or butter
3 tablespoons flour
1½ cups sweet milk
½ teaspoon salt
⅛ teaspoon pepper
½ teaspoon Worcestershire sauce
2 hard boiled eggs (chopped)

Melt oleo over medium heat in saucepan, add flour and stir until well blended. Add milk and seasonings and cook until thickened, stirring constantly. Add chopped hard boiled eggs and serve hot over the salmon roll.

This is delicious and is a one dish meal in itself if served with a green salad. Makes a nice Lenten dish also.
Submitted by Irma W. Benner, South Harpswell, Maine

Potted Mackerel Or Herring

Fish
¼ cup salt
½ cup sugar

1 teaspoon pepper
3 teaspoons cinnamon
Vinegar to cover

Place fish in a 2-quart bean pot or baking dish. Add salt, sugar and spices. Cover with vinegar (part water may be used). Bake for 3 hours in a 300 degree oven. The fish will cook up like salmon — the bones will be soft.

No reason why other kinds of fish couldn't be cooked in the same way. This I used when we had tinker mackerel.
Submitted by Mrs. Albert J. Austin, South Brooksville, Maine

Jellied Fish Salad

1 envelope unflavored gelatin
¼ cup cold water
¾ cup boiled salad dressing
½ teaspoon salt
¼ teaspoon paprika
Dash cayenne

1 tablespoon mild vinegar
1 cup flaked fish*
½ cup chopped celery
¼ cup chopped green pepper
2 tablespoons chopped olives

Soften gelatin in cold water; dissolve over hot water; cool. Add salad dressing, salt, paprika, cayenne and vinegar. Chill until slightly thickened, fold in remaining ingredients. Turn into individual molds; chill until firm. Unmold and serve on nests of lettuce leaves, garnish with slices of stuffed olives. Serves 4-6.
*Use tuna, salmon, crabmeat or any cooked flaked fish.
Submitted by Jannie H. Wiers, St. Albans, Maine

Jellied Salmon Salad

2 cups flaked salmon
1 tablespoon plain gelatin
¼ cup cold water
2 teaspoons butter
1 tablespoon flour
1½ tablespoons sugar

1 teaspoon dry mustard
Salt and pepper to taste
2 egg yolks
¾ cup milk
¼ cup vinegar

113

continued

SPICY SOLE serves family or company. (Recipe on Page 118)

Soften gelatine in the cold water. In a double boiler melt the butter, add flour, sugar, mustard, salt and pepper, blend well. Stir in egg yolks (beaten slightly) and the milk; mix well. Add vinegar slowly, stirring constantly. Cook until mixture thickens. Stir in gelatine and salmon. Spoon into a mold. Chill until set.

Submitted by Ruth Savage, Palmyra, Maine

Salmon Mold

1 package lemon gelatin
1 pint hot water
3 tablespoons vinegar
½ teaspoon salt
4 teaspoons drained
  horseradish

1 cup flaked salmon
1 cup cooked peas, fresh or
  canned
1 cup cooked diced carrots

Dissolve gelatin in hot water, add vinegar and ¼ teaspoon salt. Pour small amount of gelatin in bottom of loaf pan, chill until firm. Chill remaining gelatin until slightly thickened. Add ¼ teaspoon salt and horseradish to salmon and vegetables and mix very lightly. When remaining gelatin is slightly thickened, fold in fish and vegetable mixture. Turn into loaf pan over firm gelatin layer. Chill until firm. Unmold and cut in squares. Serve on crisp lettuce. Garnish with mayonnaise and sprigs of parsley. Serves 8.

Submitted by Myrtle S. MacLauchlan, Ripley, Maine

Salmon Sauce

When I was a boy and living in Beachmont, Mass., it was traditional to have "salmon" and green peas for 4th of July dinner (I am now 87).

My mother would wrap a nice piece of fish in cheesecloth, putting it to boil with peppercorns, a bay leaf and some salt. When properly cooked the salmon was served with a sauce made of melted butter and regular "hot dog mustard" thoroughly stirred together.

I often make this sauce when I boil other fish and it really does taste good.

Submitted by Armin "Gus" Hauck, Waldoboro, Maine

Seafood Souffle

2 cups flaked salmon, tuna
   or cut-up shrimp
1 tablespoon lemon juice
4 tablespoons butter or oleo
4 tablespoons flour
½ teaspoon salt
1 cup milk
3 eggs, separated
¼ teaspoon cream of tartar

Sprinkle lemon juice over fish. Melt butter, blend in flour, add salt and stir in the milk. Cook over low heat until thickened, about 5 minutes, stirring constantly. Stir in the prepared seafood, remove from heat and stir in slowly the 3 egg yolks, beaten until lemon colored. Beat the egg whites until frothy, add the cream of tartar and continue beating until stiff enough to hold a point. Fold carefully into seafood mixture. Pour carefully into a well-greased 8-inch casserole (1½ quart-size) and set in a pan of hot water to bake. The souffle will puff way up and become golden on top. When done it is set so a silver knife cut into center comes out clean. Bake about 35 minutes in a 350 degree oven.

Submitted by Lulu M. Miller, Waldoboro, Maine

Salmon Loaf

1 cup flaked cooked salmon
   (canned is good)
1 cup bread crumbs
1 cup milk
1 teaspoon salt
1 tablespoon butter
1 teaspoon grated onion
2 eggs

Separate the eggs. Soak bread crumbs in the milk. Combine salmon with crumbs, salt, butter, and onion. Add the egg yolks. Beat the egg whites stiff and fold in last. Pour in a greased casserole and bake for 1 hour at 350 degrees.

Submitted by Mrs. Crosby Prior, Friendship, Maine

Salmon Loaf

2 cups flaked, cooked salmon
3 tablespoons flour
3 tablespoons fat
Seasoning
1 cup milk and salmon liquid
2 cups bread cubes
1 egg, well beaten

Make a sauce by blending fat and flour, add milk and stir into fat mixture slowly. Cook until thickened. Mix sauce with salmon, bread cubes and beaten egg. Pour into a greased casserole and bake uncovered for ½ hour at 350 degrees.

Submitted Juanita Jones, Auburn, Maine

Tuna Or Salmon Biscuit Loaf

1 cup tuna or 1½ cups salmon, flaked
¼ cup chopped onion
1 cup well drained cooked lima beans, or green beans, or peas
½ to 1 teaspoon salt
¼ teaspoon pepper
1 cup diced American cheese
2 tablespoons chopped pimento

Mix above ingredients together and let stand while making biscuit dough as follows:

2 cups flour
1 teaspoon salt
3 teaspoons baking powder
⅓ cup vegetable oil
⅔ cup milk

Sift together the flour, salt and baking powder. Put into one cup but do not stir the oil and milk. Pour all at once into flour mixture, stir with fork, smooth by kneading dough. Roll out between waxed paper into a 10 x 12 inch rectangle. Place on ungreased cooky sheet. Spread filling down center of dough; cover and seal in with dough, cutting indentation for slices. Bake 20 to 25 minutes at 425 degrees. Serve at once with Mushroom-Vegetable Sauce.

Mushroom-Vegetable Sauce

Saute ½ cup of onion in ¼ cup of butter until golden, about 5 minutes. Add 1 cup sliced fresh mushrooms and continue to saute for 3 or 4 minutes. Remove from heat and add 3 tablespoons flour, stirring until smooth, then gradually add 1½ cups milk. Cook over medium heat until thickened. Add salt and pepper to taste and 1 cup of drained cooked green peas or mixed vegetables.

Submitted by Terry N. Dodge, Cushing, Maine

Elegant Fillet Of Sole

Place fresh or thawed frozen fillets in greased baking dish. Dot with butter, add salt and pepper to taste, and cook 10 minutes in 300 degree oven. Remove fish from oven and spread with sauce of sour cream and Parmesan cheese. Bake an additional 25 minutes at 350 degrees. (Sauce proportions should equal about 8 ounces sour cream to 3 ounces Parmesan cheese.)

Submitted by Eleanor C. Linton, Camden, Maine

Crispy Fried Fillet of Sole

1½ pounds sole fillets, cut in serving pieces
⅓ cup flour
½ cup cracker crumbs
1 egg, whipped lightly with a little water (egg wash)
Salt to taste, add to cracker crumbs or egg wash
Oil for frying

Roll the fillets one by one in the flour, patting it in well. Dip them into egg wash and then roll in cracker crumbs. Fry in the hot oil, turning once. Add a bit of new oil for the second pan.

I usually cook the sole in an electric frying pan in cooking oil about 1⅛" deep at 380 degrees, turning it once when it is a delicate brown on one side.

Serve with tartar sauce. Serves 4 or 5.

Submitted by Norman C. Perkins, Bangor Maine

Spicy Sole

1 cup water
¼ bay leaf
1 vegetable, chicken or beef cube
½ teaspoon salt
6 peppercorns
Pinch thyme
3 inch strip lemon peel
4 medium fillets of sole
4½ teaspoons margarine
4½ teaspoons flour
¾ cup poaching liquid
Dash red pepper
Dash onion powder
½ cup cooked shrimp

Combine water with next 6 ingredients in skillet and heat to simmer over low heat. Fold fillets of sole in half, crosswise, and place in simmering liquid, cover and cook 10 minutes, or until fish flakes easily when tested with fork. Remove fish from liquid with slotted spoon. Strain liquid into measuring cup. Melt margarine in saucepan over low heat, then stir in flour. Add poaching liquid gradually and cook until mixture boils and is thickened, stir in the red pepper, seasoning and onion powder.

Cut 4 sheets aluminum foil 9 x 12 inches and trim to heart shape. Place 1 tablespoon sauce, then place shrimp on fillets. Pour remaining sauce over fish. Close foil, making double fold around edges. Place on baking sheet. Bake in moderate oven (350 degrees) 10 minutes. Serve in foil, slashing open with knife. Makes 4 servings.

Submitted by Mrs. Evelyn Wishart, Sanford, Maine

PERCH IN CREAMY GARLIC SAUCE is savory but economical for gourmet meals. (Recipe on Page 121)

Freshwater Fish

Many freshwater fish, including much trout, are raised in modern hatcheries and fish farms, using scientific equipment and creating fast-growing healthy fish. Many of this type of fish which were native to the Pacific coast have since been transplanted in nearly every state in the Union. Conversely, Eastern fish have also traveled West. Smelt from Green Lake in Maine were transplanted in Crystal Lake, Michigan, in 1906. And now that lake is well populated with smelt.

Among the best fresh water fish caught in Maine are bass, pickerel, smelt, trout (brook), trout (lakers), yellow perch, white perch, and eels.

Baked Black Bass

Have the fish nicely cleaned, rub well with bread crumbs, sprinkle with salt. Lay several pieces of onion and small bits of butter over and inside the fish. Bake from one-half to three-quarters of an hour in a moderate oven. Garnish with lettuce leaves.

Taken from "The Economist," a Practicel Common Sence
Cook Book printed in 1906 by
The Advertiser Press in Pittsfield, Maine

Baked Striped Bass Fillets

Take fish fillets and put them in a baking dish. I use a cookie sheet covered with foil. Brush with a mixture of melted margarine, lemon juice and A-1 sauce. Bake about 45 minutes at 350 degrees (longer for a large fish).

Submitted by Mrs. Eugene Doran, Rockland, Maine

Baked Alewives

Wipe whole alewives with damp cloth after entrails have been removed. Lay on heavy duty aluminum foil in baking pan. Brush with olive oil. Pour fresh lemon juice over fish. Bake for 5 hours at 275 degrees. Remove skin and what bones are left. Delicious.

Submitted by Myrtle Achorn, Waldoboro, Maine

Baked Eels

Skin 4 eels and cut into 3 pieces each. Roll in flour, season with salt and pepper and dot with butter. Place on greased baking sheet or shallow pan. Bake in moderately hot 375 degree oven for about 20 minutes. Serve while hot. 6 servings.
Submitted by Blanche K. Wallace, Friendship, Maine

Baked Eels

Skin the eels, split them and remove backbone. Cut in 2 or 3 inch pieces. Wash in salted water and dry thoroughly. Dredge with flour and season with salt and pepper. Place in a buttered baking pan and add about a half cup of water to prevent burning. Cover and bake in a 400 degree oven for 15-20 minutes or until eel is browned.

Fried Eels

Skin eels, split them lengthwise and remove the bone. Cut the strips into 3-inch lengths. Dredge with salt and pepper. Dip each piece in beaten egg and then in cornmeal. Drop them in hot fat and fry about 5 minutes.
Submitted by Eva Meservey, Jefferson, Maine

Perch With Creamy Garlic Sauce

2 pounds perch or other fish fillets
¾ cup dry white wine or water
1 small onion, sliced
1 small bay leaf
1¼ teaspoons salt
½ teaspoon tarragon (measure carefully, a little goes a long way)
1 clove garlic, minced
½ teaspoon dry mustard
¼ teaspoon black pepper
1 cup salad dressing or mayonnaise
1 tablespoon lemon juice
2 packages (10 oz. each) frozen broccoli spears or equivalent fresh
Paprika or chopped parsley (optional)

121 continued

Thaw fish if frozen. Cook and drain the frozen broccoli spears. Combine water or wine, onion, bay leaf, 1 teaspoon salt, and tarragon in a skillet. Bring to a boil and simmer for 5 minutes. Add fillets, cover and simmer for 8 minutes or until fish flakes easily. Drain and save liquid. To prepare sauce: Combine garlic, mustard, pepper and ¼ teaspoon salt. Mash together until smooth. Stir in salad dressing or mayonnaise and lemon juice. Strain the fish liquid and stir ¼ to ½ cup into the sauce until desired consistency. Arrange the hot cooked, drained broccoli spears on a heated platter and place hot drained fillets on top of spears. Spoon sauce over top of fish and broccoli. Sprinkle with paprika or parsley. Serves 6.

National Marine Fisheries Service,
U. S. Department of Commerce

Oven-Fried Lake Perch For Twenty-five

25 lake perch fillets (4 oz. each)   1 cup milk
  fresh or frozen   1 pint toasted bread crumbs
1½ teaspoons salt   ½ cup melted fat or oil

Thaw fillets if frozen. Divide into 25 portions. Add salt to the milk. Dip fillets into milk, then roll in crumbs, using a small amount at a time. Place a single layer in a well-greased baking pan. Pour fat or oil over the fish. Bake at 500 degrees about 15 to 20 minutes or until fish is brown and flakes easily when tested with a fork.

Bureau of Commercial Fisheries, U. S. Dept. of the Interior

Broiled Pickerel
(This is also good for small lake salmon or trout.)

Take head off fish, clean, leaving the tail on. Split the fish open, place skin down and lay a strip of bacon on each section of the flesh. Place under the broiler and cook for about 10 minutes until fish is done (bacon will get very crisp and dark). Fish need not be turned over. Sprinkle with a little lemon juice and serve.

Submitted by Mrs. Terry Dodge, Cushing, Maine

122

Baked Stuffed Pickerel

2½ to 3-pound pickerel, dressed

3 cups bread crumbs

3 slices of bacon, cut in small pieces

3 tablespoons melted butter

½ cup celery, cut in small pieces

2 tablespoons chopped onion

Dash flaked parsley

Lemon juice, salt, pepper

Rub the inside of fish with lemon juice, salt and pepper. Make a dressing with the bread brumbs, melted butter, celery, onion and parsley. Mix well. Stuff fish with the dressing and score the fish three times and place bacon on the fish. Place fish in a greased pan, uncovered and bake about 1½ hours in a 350 degree oven. When done, place fish on a warmed platter with lemon slices and olives surrounding it. If fish seems dry on the outside, rub it with a little lemon butter mixture. To conserve fuel, bake some potatoes along with it.

Submitted by Mrs. J. Warren Everett, Thomaston, Maine

Baked Pickerel

Clean the fish and wipe dry. Rub cavity with salt. Fill with dill stuffing (or your favorite recipe), place strips of salt pork over the fish.

Line a shallow pan with foil, grease it lightly, lay the fish in and bake at 350 degrees until the fish flakes easily.

Garnish with fresh dill sprigs or parsley if available, and serve with cucumber salad and sour cream dressing.

(It's always a good idea to line a metal pan with foil, if you don't want fishy flavors to linger. Besides, it helps to lift the fish out to the serving platter without breaking.)

Dill Stuffing

3 cups soft bread crumbs

½ teaspoon salt

⅛ teaspoon pepper

3 tablespoons minced onion

⅓ cup melted butter or margarine

¼ cup celery, chopped very fine

¼ cup chopped dill pickle

2 tablespoons chopped parsley

Mix bread crumbs with seasonings and onion, add butter slowly and toss lightly until mixed. Add pickle and mix again. This makes quite a bit of stuffing, enough for several fish.

Submitted by Mrs. Ivy Dodd, Thomaston, Maine

Poached Lake Salmon

Put enough water as will cover fish in a stainless steel skillet or other pan with some bay leaves and celery leaves, salt and a few peppercorns or coarsely cracked pepper. Simmer for five or 10 minutes. Clean, behead and wash fish and cut tail off if too long for the pan. Lay fish gently in the liquid, cover and poach for about 10 minutes until the flesh flakes easily. Serve with melted butter mixed with a little lemon juice, and with lemon wedges.

Submitted by Mrs. Rose Wales, Cushing, Maine

Pickled Salmon

4 slices fresh salmon
2 cups water
2 sliced onions
½ cup sugar

1½ cups vinegar
½ teaspoon salt
2 teaspoons pickling spice
1 hot red chili pepper*

Put water, onions and salt into a deep saucepan. Bring to a boil. Add the salmon and boil for 20 minutes. Remove salmon to a deep bowl. To the sauce from the fish add the vinegar, sugar, pepper, and spices. Boil for 5 minutes. Strain and pour over the salmon. Cool, cover and place in refrigerator to use when needed.

*(If I don't want to buy a whole lot I pick one out from a jar of pickles I might have on hand.)

Submitted by Mary W. Sibo, Old Town Maine

Chesuncook Special

1 three-pound salmon*
1½ cups bread crumbs
2 tablespoons melted butter
¼ teaspoon salt
Pepper

1 teaspoon minced onion
1 can minced clams
1 teaspoon lemon juice
1 can cream of shrimp soup

Place fish in a greased baking dish. To prepare stuffing, mix bread crumbs, melted butter, salt, pepper, onion, minced clams and juice, and the lemon juice. Mix well. Wipe the inside of fish dry and stuff. Dilute the cream of shrimp soup with ¼ cup of water and pour over the fish, letting some go over the stuffing. Bake at 350 degrees for about 40 minutes.

The title of this recipe is taken from Chesuncook Lake up near Ripogenus Dam, where we have been lucky enough to catch a few fish.

*(If you are lucky enough to catch a larger one, that is all right, too; or 2 trout may be used.)

Submitted by Mrs. Joan Caron, Old Town, Maine

124

Baked Smelts

Medium-sized smelts
1 cup cracker meal
Salt, pepper

¼ pound butter or margarine
2 tablespoons bacon grease

Melt fat in skillet on medium heat, roll fish in meal with salt and pepper. Cook on both sides until done.

Can cook fish covered in a 400 degree oven until half done, then take cover off and finish cooking to let fish brown.

Submitted by Mrs. Myrtle E. Nord, Fairhaven, Mass.
(Formerly from Friendship, Maine)

Baked Smelts

Clean fish and cut off heads, wipe with damp towel, do not wash. Dip first into milk, then into a mixture of cornmeal and mixed herbs. Place on a well-greased dish or cookie sheet and drizzle oil over. Bake until done, but don't overbake.

Good if you've a lot of smelts and a number of mouths to feed all at once, and we prefer this method to frying.

Submitted by Ivy Dodd, Thomaston, Maine

Fried Smelts

Cut heads off back of gill, open fish and clean. Wipe with a dry cloth. Dip in a mixture of equal parts of flour and cornmeal with a dash of salt added. Fry in hot pork fat. Drain and serve hot.

Taken from Sebasticook Grange, Newport 1975 Cookbook.

Fried Smelts

Clean smelts (do not remove heads), and wipe with a damp cloth. Sprinkle with salt and pepper and roll in cracker meal. Melt butter and bacon fat in skillet (heat but do not allow fat to smoke). Fry smelts 3 minutes on one side or until a golden brown, turn with spatula. Add a little more butter if necessary and brown quickly another 2 minutes or until crisp on the outside, but juicy when opened with fork.

Submitted by Mrs. Myrtle E. Nord, Fairhaven, Mass.
(Formerly of Maine)

CAMPFIRE FISH for outdoor appetites! (Recipe on Page 127)

Smelt Sandwiches

1 pound pan-dressed smelt or
other small fish, fresh or
frozen
1 egg, beaten
1 tablespoon milk
1 cup dry bread crumbs

2 teaspoons paprika
2 teaspoons dried thyme
½ teaspoon salt
6 hot dog rolls, heated
Tartar sauce

Thaw fish if frozen; clean, wash and dry fresh fish. Combine beaten egg' and milk. Combine the crumbs with paprika, thyme and salt. Dip fish in egg mixture and roll in crumb mixture. Place in a single layer in a fry basket. Fry in deep fat (350 degrees) for 2 to 3 minutes or until brown and fish flakes easily when tested with a fork. Drain on absorbent paper. Spread the hot dog rolls with tartar sauce. Place 3 or 4 fried fish in each roll. Serve with more sauce. Serves 6.

Bureau of Commercial Fisheries, U. S. Dept. of Interior

Campfire Fish

Catch a fish! Clean it, leaving the head on. Wash it, leaving it damp, season with salt.

Take a piece of maple about four inches through, split it down the center.

Open up the fish flat and nail it to the split side of the wood. At the top of the head, hang a piece of bacon. Stand the fish in front of the fire, tail down, to cook — time will depend on the size of the fish. When the fish is done, push the flesh off with a fork right into your pan or plate, leaving the skin just where it is. Proceed to eat!

———

If you'll be staying at a campsite all day, dig three holes in the ground — one for breakfast, one for noon and one for supper. The size of the holes will depend on the size of the fish you've managed to catch.

Clean the fish, wash it and place it in foil. Slit the skin of a whole, unpeeled potato and wrap it up with the fish in the foil. The potato takes the muddy taste out of the fish such as perch, or bass late in the season.

Come mealtime, build a fire over the holes which have been covered with earth about two inches deep. Fish usually will take about an hour to cook.

continued

Let the fire go down, dig the fish out, throw away the potato and satisfy your appetite with the fish.

Throw the whole thing away and start all over if you've forgotten to slit the potato and it's burst inside the foil!

Submitted by Roy B. Gardner, Warren, Maine
("The Coastal Outdoorsman" columnist for The Courier-Gazette)

Brook Trout — Camper's Delight

First catch the fish! Split open, take head off and clean thoroughly. Shake dry and dust with flour. Throw into a skillet with a little hot bacon fat or butter in it. Fry until skin is crisp and the fish flakes easily with a fork. Salt to taste.

Submitted by Mrs. Beverly A. Nelson, Rockland, Maine

Broiled Trout

Brush trout with oil, salt and pepper them. Broil 3 or 4 inches from heat for eight minutes on each side. Fish should be browned and flake easily with a fork. Serve with lemon wedges and parsley for garnish.

Broiled or baked trout is good served with a caper sauce made from a knob of butter, a little flour, 1 teaspoon of lemon juice, 1 dessertspoon of capers and a little fish stock. Cream the butter and flour, pour on hot liquid, stir until it boils and becomes smooth, then add the capers, lemon juice and salt and white pepper to taste. (If you add a little anchovy paste it will add a great deal to the sauce but since it is so salty, you won't need to add any extra salt to season.) Simmer for a few minutes, then pour over fish to serve.

Submitted by Mrs. Ivy Dodd, Thomaston, Maine

Poached Lake Trout

Place fish in skillet or long pan. Combine half a cup of milk and half a cup of water with four slices of lemon, ½ teaspoon allspice, ½ teaspoon salt and a sprig of parsley. Pour over fish and cook over a low heat for 20 minutes or until just tender.

Submitted by Helen Barnes, Rockland, Maine

128

Trout or Salmon

2½ to 3-pound trout or
  salmon
1 quart of cold water
1 medium onion
1 large carrot

2 tablespoons chopped parsley
1 tablespoon vinegar or lemon
  juice
2½ teaspoons salt

Clean the fish, bone if desired, then wrap in cheesecloth. Put water in a pan large enough to lay whole fish in straight. Add onion, carrot, parsley, vinegar or lemon juice and salt. Heat water to boiling and boil gently for 10 minutes. Place fish in the liquid and simmer gently about ½ hour or until fish is tender, but firm. Cool thoroughly in the liquid and place in the refrigerator as soon as practical after removing from the heat. Before serving, remove fish from the liquid to a platter and carefully remove the cheesecloth and all skin. Pour relish dressing or sour cream sauce over fish when served. Serves 4.

Submitted by Mrs. Claire Dumont, Orono, Maine

"Fish On The Rocks"

Small fish or fish fillets
Thinly sliced onions
Butter or margarine

Salt, pepper and paprika
Heavy duty aluminum foil

Wash and clean fish. Place fish on large piece of aluminum foil. Place thinly sliced onions (or onion powder), pats of butter or margarine, salt, pepper and paprika on each fish. Then carefully wrap each fish tightly in the foil. Place over hot coals on the barbecue. After about 10 minutes, check to see if the fish flakes. If not, leave on grill a few minutes more.

You will find this an easy and tasty dish at a barbecue and guests will enjoy making up their own package to grill. Just have lots of fish on hand.

Submitted by Irene M. Petzolt, Long Island, New York

Poor Man's Lobster

1 pound pollock
  (fresh or frozen)
1½ quarts water

1 tablespoon salt
½ stick butter, melted
Dash of vinegar

Boil the pollock in water in which the salt has been added until it turns a white gray (no longer translucent). Drain. Serve with the melted butter mixed with the vinegar. You can't tell the difference from the real thing. Serves 2.

Submitted by Abigail Ritter Wade, Lubec, Maine

CODFISH CAKES are a tradition, with fresh or salt cod.
(Recipe on Page 135)

Salt Fish

All kinds of fish have been cured by a salting process applied to varieties caught in lakes and rivers as well as those caught in the ocean.

The three methods most often used are "dry salting," "wet salting" and "mild salted" or "corned." For dry salting, alternate layers of fish and salt are placed in large containers where they will make a pickle. Here they remain for three weeks. They are removed from the pickle and dried, skinned and boned and packed for the retailer. These are lean species of fish.

Fish containing large amounts of fat are wet salted, just about the same way as for dry salting. However, after being thoroughly salted or pickled they cannot be dried and sold because the oxygen of the air will "burn" the fish and fat, giving it a strong taste, liked by the "old-timers" but not preferred by the fish-eating public today. All salted fish of the fat varieties are sold in watertight containers which keeps the product away from the air and in prime condition.

Mild salted or corned fish are really fish which have been left in the pickle for a day or two. These are much liked in many sections of the country, as they are not so salty and lend themselves to quicker preparation.

The modern method for freshening salt fish is as follows: Place the fish in a large amount of water and over the hottest burner of the stove. Bring this water almost to a boil, but not quite. Drain and refill with cold water. Repeat this process three or four times. Test to indicate if fish is just right for your taste. By this process the fish will be tender and all ready to serve on a hot platter with white sauce or your favorite boiled potatoes and pork scraps.

Salt fish of all kinds and varieties after freshening can be baked, broiled, fried, boiled or used in many of your everyday recipes.

Old-Fashioned Salt Fish, Potatoes And Gravy

1 pound dry salt cod, or any
   salt fish
¼ to ½ pound salt fat pork
Boiled potatoes (use desired
   amount)

¼ cup vinegar
¼ cup water
1 teaspoon sugar
1 large onion

Soak salt fish in cold water to cover, overnight. Boil the desired amount of potatoes. Dice the salt pork and fry out until pork is crisp. Keep warm, as this is the gravy. Drain fish, cover again with water and bring to a boil and cook slowly for 12 to 15 minutes.

A few hours before serving, prepare the following: Mix the vinegar with the water and sugar. Cut up onion in vinegar mixture, and let marinate in the refrigerator for 2 hours or more.

Drain the fish and serve over potatoes and top with the marinated onion and the salt pork gravy (fat and scraps).

Submitted by Mrs. Irving H. Parsons, Stockton Springs, Maine

Corned Hake

10 pounds dressed hake
1 cup rock salt

Water to cover

Put hake in a stone crock with the salt and water to cover. Set in a cool place for 2 or 3 days. To cook, drain water from the hake and rinse off surplus salt. Cover with water and bring to boil. Cook for ½ hour or until done. Flake and remove the bones. Serve on boiled potatoes with a pitcher or bowl of salt pork fat and the little crisp pieces of pork remaining. Buttered beets go well with this.

This was a favorite meal with my family. Grampa Joy always seemed to have a stone crock of hake corning in the boat house and grandma did a great job of serving it up with hot biscuits and some kind of pie. I seem to remember her apple or mince the best.

Submitted by Mrs. Inga J. Chase, Camden, Maine

Corned Hake, Potatoes And Pork Scraps

5-pound hake (head removed)
or
3 pounds of hake fillets
3 tablespoons salt per pound of fish
2 medium potatoes for each serving

½ pound fat-back salt pork
2 or 3 medium-sized white onions, thinly sliced
⅓ cup salad oil
½ cup vinegar
Salt and pepper

Place fish in a dish and sprinkle freely with the salt. Cover and place in the refrigerator until ready to use (2 or 3 days), or if heavily salted, can use the next day.

To cook the fish, place in a large kettle with water to nearly cover, bring to a boil and gently simmer for about 20 minutes or until fish flakes easily with a fork.

Boil at least 2 medium potatoes for each serving. While fish and potatoes are cooking, thinly slice the salt pork and fry over medium heat until lightly browned and crisp.

One last ingredient of this meal is thinly sliced white onions. Mix the salad oil, vinegar, salt and pepper. Cover onions with this mixture and place in refrigerator for a while. These can be done earlier.

To eat: Mash potatoes and fish together, add a couple of pork scraps, and a couple spoonfuls of pork fat. Mix all together, add a few onions to your plate and enjoy a most delicious "corned hake supper."

Submitted by Kay Dodge, Owls Head, Maine

Codfish Balls

3 cups diced potato
2½ cups flaked codfish
  (1 pound package)

2 tablespoons butter
½ teaspoon pepper
2 eggs, slightly beaten

Freshen salt codfish according to package directions. Cook potatoes and fish in boiling water until tender. Drain thoroughly. Mash and add butter, egg and pepper. Beat until light; shape into balls or drop from spoon into deep fat, 375 degrees. Fry golden brown and drain on soft crumpled paper. Makes 6 servings.

Submitted by Elsie Swanson, Ellsworth, Maine

Creamed Salt Codfish

1 package (about 1 pound)	2 cups milk or half and half
dried salt codfish	1/4 cup flour
1/2 stick butter or margarine	Salt and pepper to taste

Let codfish freshen in cold water for several hours or overnight. Drain, place in cold water over low heat and let it heat, but do not simmer. Drain fish and flake into bite-size pieces. Melt butter in a saucepan and stir in flour to make a smooth mixture. Add milk slowly and bring to a boil, stir constantly. Cook until thickened. Season with salt and pepper to taste. Add codfish and a little more butter.

Makes a good supper dish with new potatoes and green beans.

Submitted by Loana S. Shibles, Palmyra, Maine

Codfish Cakes

2 cups salt codfish	1/4 cup milk
2 cups hot mashed potatoes	1/2 teaspoon baking powder
1 tablespoon butter	Dash of pepper

Soak codfish for 2 hours in cold water. Drain. Then cover with fresh cold water and put on low heat and simmer until fish is tender. Drain fish and chop fine. Mix milk, butter, baking powder and pepper thoroughly with mashed potatoes, add codfish and beat well. Shape into flat cakes and fry in butter or bacon fat.

Submitted by Clara W. Thornton, North Haven, Maine

Codfish Pie

Flake not too small some freshened and simmered salt codfish and put a layer in bottom of a baking dish. Season with a little pepper and small bits of butter. Cover this with a layer of sliced potatoes that have been half cooked and some minced onion; dust a little flour on each layer. Add seasoning as before, another layer of fish, etc. Let the last layer be of sliced hard-cooked eggs. Pour in enough hot milk to cover and put over all a rich biscuit crust and bake slowly about 40 minutes.

Copied from a cookbook by the Congregational Ladies of Houlton around 1900.

Submitted by Lulu M. Miller, Waldoboro, Maine

Codfish Fritters

Strips of salt cod
2 level tablespoons flour
1 egg, separated

⅓ cup milk
Fat for frying

Cut fish into strips about the size of the finger and soak overnight. Drain and dry. Make a batter by putting the flour into a bowl, add the yolk of the egg and the milk. Beat well to remove lumps. Beat white of egg to a stiff froth, add to the batter and dip the strips of fish into it, one at a time. Drop at once into the hot fat, having enough fat in the pan to completely cover the fritters. Cook golden brown and drain well before serving.

Submitted by Athelene Hilt, Union, Maine

Herring Cakes
(Sill Bullar)

1 salt herring
5 or 6 medium-sized potatoes, cooked

1 egg, beaten
Flour and butter

Soak herring in water overnight. Remove skin and bones and chop fine. Mash the cooked potatoes and mix well with the herring. Add the beaten egg. Shape into cakes, roll in flour and fry in butter. Serve hot with currant sauce.

Currant Sauce

3 tablespoons dry currants
3 cups water
1 tablespoon butter

2 tablespoons flour
1 tablespoon vinegar
Sugar and salt to taste

Wash and clean currants and cook in water until soft.
Make a sauce of the flour, butter and currant water. Cook for 10 minutes. Add vinegar, salt and sugar. Serves 6.

Submitted by Julia Burgess, Waldoboro, Maine
(This is my Swedish mother's recipe.)

Pickled Herring

2 salt herring
1 large onion, thinly sliced
1 cup cider vinegar

1 cup water
1 tablespoon allspice berries
1 large bay leaf

Soak in cold water for 3 hours the herring which has been cleaned and cut into fillets.

Drain herring and cut into 2-inch square pieces. Put a layer of herring into a shallow bowl and top with some of the onion rings. Repeat layers of herring and onions. Mix together the vinegar and water with the spices. Pour this over the herring and onion. Chill thoroughly several hours or overnight to blend flavors. A "must" for the smorgasbord.

Submitted by Edith Holmstrom, St. George, Maine

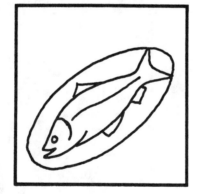

FINNAN HADDIE CASSEROLE is a new way of serving the dried, smoked fish

Smoked Fish

Mild smoked fish is not a product that will keep and should be treated as fresh fish. Smoked fillets, finnan haddie, etc., are delightful products and should form a definite part of the menu.

Hard smoked fish such as bloater herring, kippers, smoked salt salmon and smoked sturgeon can be skinned and eaten as they are, cold, because they are smoked under heated conditions which accomplish cooking. If they are to be further cooked, soak in cold water or in water and vinegar for half an hour. Cooking usually consists of placing in a pan in the oven or on top of the stove, turning the fish several times until heated through thoroughly, and usually served with eggs, boiled potatoes and vegetables. The hard smoked fish is also suitable for sandwiches, hors d'oeuvres, canapes, etc.

Broiled Finnan Haddie

2 pounds finnan haddie
Hot water

2 tablespoons butter
Pepper

Cover finnan haddie with hot water and let stand 10 minutes. Drain. Place on greased broiler rack, spread with butter, sprinkle lightly with pepper and broil in preheated broiler under moderate heat until brown, turning once. Serves 4.
Submitted by Mrs. Gloria Matthews Simmons, Rockland, Maine

Creamed Finnan Haddie

1½ pounds finnan haddie
2 tablespoons butter
1 tablespoon finely chopped onion
2 tablespoons flour
½ teaspoon salt

Dash pepper
1 cup light cream
¾ cup milk
3 chilled hard-cooked eggs
Chopped parsley

Place finnan haddie in a saucepan with water to cover; bring to a boil, then drain. Add water to cover again, bring to a boil and simmer for 15 minutes. Melt butter in a saucepan and saute onion until golden, about 5 minutes. Remove from heat, stir in flour, salt and pepper until smooth. Gradually stir in cream and milk. Cook over medium heat, stirring until thickened.

Preheat oven to 300 degrees. Drain the finnan haddie, rinse with hot water and place in oven-proof serving dish.

continued

Shell the cooled eggs, chop coarsely and place over the fish, reserving a small amount of yolk to garnish.

Pour sauce over all and bake 10 minutes. Sieve the reserved egg yolk and use with chopped parsley to garnish. Serves 4.

Great with boiled buttered new potatoes and fresh peas.

Submitted by Terry N. Dodge, NE-9, Cushing, Maine

Finnan Haddie And Potato Casserole

¾ pound finnan haddie
4 medium potatoes, pared and diced

2½ cups milk
2 tablespoons butter

Cut finnan haddie into serving size pieces and put into saucepan with potatoes and milk. Heat slowly until milk begins to simmer. Turn into a shallow baking dish and dot with butter. Bake in a moderate oven (350 degrees) until potatoes are tender, from 30 to 35 minutes. Serves 5.

Submitted by Elsie Swanson, Ellsworth, Maine

Creamed Finnan Haddie
Using leftovers

½ to ¾ of a pound finnan haddie
1 pint of milk
2 or 3 tablespoons cornstarch

4 leftover cooked potatoes, sliced
½ cup leftover peas or carrots or string beans

Boil fish in just enough water to cover and cook until it flakes. Do not drain. Add 1½ cups of milk to the fish and heat slowly. Mix cornstarch with ½ cup of milk and stir until smooth. Add slowly to the fish mixture, enough to make fish creamy. Remove from heat. Add leftover vegetables and turn into a casserole. Heat in a 325 degree oven until hot.

Submitted by Mrs. Norman E. Jones, Cushing, Maine

Baked Finnan Haddie

1 pound smoked fillets
Milk

Soak fillets in warm water for 5 minutes. Drain and rinse with cold water. Place in pan, cover with milk and bake in moderately hot (400 degree) oven for 25 to 30 minutes.

Submitted by Flora W. Wotton, Friendship, Maine

Casserole Of Finnan Haddie

1½ pounds of finnan haddie
Milk and water to cover
4 medium cooked potatoes
2 hard-cooked eggs
2 tablespoons chopped pimento
7 tablespoons margarine

4 tablespoons flour
3 cups milk
4 slices bread
3 tablespoons margarine
Salt and pepper to taste

Soak the fish for 30 minutes in half water and milk to cover. Bring to boil over low heat 15 minutes. Drain, cool and flake. In a saucepan blend flour and margarine to make a paste over low heat and gradually add the milk and seasoning. Add flaked fish, cut-up potatoes and sliced eggs. Pour into a large casserole. Cube the bread and saute in 3 tablespoons of margarine. Put on top of the casserole and bake at 350 degrees 25 to 30 minutes.
Submitted by Mrs. Charles E. McMahon, South Thomaston, Maine

Finnan Haddie Casserole

1½ pounds to 3 pounds finnan haddie
6 medium sized potatoes, sliced
2 medium sized onions, sliced
3 slices salt pork (not too fat)

2 cups water
Shake of salt and pepper
Milk, cream, butter
Paprika

In a 3-quart casserole put the finnan haddie, sliced potato and onion with slices of pork on top. Add 2 cups of water with the salt and pepper. Put cover on casserole and place in a 300 degree oven. Cook until ingredients are tender. Remove cover, put back in oven and cook until liquid is nearly cooked away. Take from oven and remove pork slices. Cover fish with milk, a bit of cream added if desired, and ⅛ pound of butter. Return to the oven until milk is hot and butter melted. Shake paprika over top sparingly, for color. Three pounds of finnan haddie cooked this way will serve 6 people.

Holler loud just once and your guests will come running. I serve old-fashioned gingerbread and whipped cream for dessert.
Submitted by Alden Ellis, Warren, Maine

QUICK CLAM CHOWDER has chicken broth for goodness. Maine is also famed for its fine poultry. (Recipe on Page 146)

Canned Fish

Today, tuna ranks No. 1 as the most popular canned seafood in the United States, with over a billion cans consumed annually. Tuna comes in solid-pack, chunk-style or grated in cans ranging from three and one-quarter ounces to 13-ounce cans.

Canned salmon can be compared with tuna in that it also is 100 percent edible, easy to store and use. Salmon comes in solid pack and in cans from three and three-quarter ounces to the four-pound cans sold to restaurants or institutions.

Next in volume sold is sardines, every one of which is canned in Maine and nowhere else in the United States. Over 135 million cans of sardines were sold in 1974 — 1,300,000 cases of 100 cans each. Sardines are packed in four-ounce cans in various types of oil as well as mustard and tomato sauces.

Many other kinds and types of seafood are canned and are well labeled with descriptions and nutritional values.

Clam Casserole

2 cans (6½ oz.) minced clams
1 can mushroom soup
1 package large soda crackers
   (crushed)

½ cup milk
Small piece of butter
   (melted)

Mix and place in buttered casserole. Sprinkle with cracker crumbs or corn flake crumbs and dot with butter. Bake at 375 degrees for 10 minutes than turn heat back to 350 degrees and bake 50 minutes longer.

Submitted by Helen L. Hallowell, Tenants Harbor, Maine

Clam Casserole

2 cups of milk
2 cups crumbled crackers
2 cans minced clams (8 oz. each)

4 eggs, beaten
¼ cup minced onions
Salt and pepper to taste

Pour milk over crackers and let stand several minutes. Add other ingredients including the clam broth.

Pour into greased 2-quart casserole. Bake in 350 degree oven 45 minutes or until set.

Submitted by Rose L. Wales, Cushing, Maine

Clam Casserole

2 cans minced clams with juice
1 can mushroom soup
1 small box salted crackers
(crumbled)

½ cup milk
1 teaspoon butter

Mix together first four ingredients and pour into a greased casserole. Put a few cracker crumbs on the top and dot with the butter. Bake at 350 degrees for an hour.

Submitted by Ms. M. K. Rollins, Abbot Village, Maine

Clam Casserole

20 salted crackers, crushed
2 cans minced clams, juice included
2 beaten eggs

1¼ cups milk
¼ cup melted butter
Salt and pepper

Mix melted butter with the crackers, then mix all together. Bake in 1½-quart casserole 40 minutes in a 350 degree oven.

Submitted by Mrs. Elizabeth Shyne, Rockland, Maine

A Quick Clam Casserole

1 can clam chowder
1 can minced clams

Heat in baking dish. While heating make biscuits, cut each one in half and place cut side down around casserole. Bake until biscuits are brown.

Submitted by Lulu M. Miller, Waldoboro, Maine

Clam Casserole

2 eggs, beaten
1 can cream of mushroom soup
30 salted crackers, crushed
1 cup milk

1 can minced clams
  with juice
¼ cup melted butter or
  margarine

Beat eggs slightly, add soup, crackers and milk. Mix well, then add the clams and the butter. Turn into a greased 1½-quart dish. Bake at 350 degrees for 1 hour.

Submitted by Mrs. Austin W. Miller, Friendship, Maine

Clam Casserole

2 eggs
1 can condensed cream of
  mushroom soup
1 (7¾ oz.) can minced clams,
  drained

2 cups oyster crackers
  (crushed)
½ cup butter or margarine,
  melted

Beat eggs and soup together. Add clams, a little more than half of the crackers. Mix well and put into a greased one quart casserole. Spread rest of crackers on top. Bake at 400 degrees about 25 minutes. Serves 4.

Submitted by Dolores Reglin, Orrington, Maine

Clam-Corn Casserole

15 to 20 crackers, broken
2 eggs, beaten
1¼ cups milk
1 can minced clams (4 oz.)
1 cup whole kernel corn
3 tablespoons onion, chopped

1 tablespoon green pepper,
  chopped
½ teaspoon salt
½ teaspoon Worcestershire
  sauce
Grated cheese

Mix together the crackers, beaten eggs and milk. Set aside to allow crackers to soften. Combine next six ingredients and add to first mixture, blending well. Pour into a greased casserole, sprinkle grated cheese over top and bake at 350 degrees for about ¾ to 1 hour until tests done.

Submitted by Mrs. Athleen Damon, Warren, Maine

Clam And Pepper Casserole

In a casserole mix together

2 cans minced clams, including juice
1 green pepper, cut fine
2 eggs, beaten

30 single crackers, broken up fine
¼ cup butter, melted
1½ cups milk

Set casserole in a pan of water and bake at 350 degrees for 50 minutes.

Submitted by Mrs. Dorothy Robbins, Ellsworth, Maine

Scalloped Corn And Minced Clam Casserole

1 can minced clams (8 oz.)
1¼ cups crushed crackers
1 onion, diced

2 eggs, beaten
1 cup milk
1 cup cream corn

Combine eggs with milk, corn and clams. Mix well. Add crushed crackers and diced onion. Pour into a greased casserole. Bake at 350 degrees for ½ hour.

Submitted by Corinne W. Small, Damariscotta, Maine

Quick Clam Chowder

1 can minced clams (7½ oz.)
1 tablespoon butter
¼ cup chopped celery
1 teaspoon minced onion
1 package (8 oz.) frozen green peas (cooked)
1 medium cooked potato, diced
2 cups medium cream sauce
1 can condensed chicken broth or 1 chicken bouillon cube dissolved in 10 oz. boiling water

⅔ cup canned milk
¼ teaspoon thyme
Salt to season
Dash of pepper
Paprika

Drain clams, reserving liquid. Cook celery and onion in butter until tender. Stir in peas, potato, cream sauce, chicken broth, canned milk, clam liquid, thyme, salt and pepper. Cook and stir until mixture starts to boil. Reduce heat, cover and simmer about 5 minutes. Stir in clams, heat to boiling point. Garnish with paprika. 4 to 6 servings.

Submitted by Mrs. Ernest Mitchell, Guilford, Maine

Clam Chowder
(For One Serving)

1 can minced clams
2 potatoes, diced
Little onion soup mix

1½ cups milk
Salt, pepper & margarine

Cook clams, potatoes and soup mix together in a small amount of water. When potatoes are tender, add the milk and seasonings.

Submitted by Mrs. Hazel Hills, Warren, Maine

Clam Cakes

1 can minced clams, drain
  (save liquid)

1 cup salted cracker crumbs
1 egg, beaten

Mix clams with cracker crumbs (I place crackers between wax paper and crush with rolling pin), add beaten egg. Shape into patties and fry in a greased frying pan. If the mixture needs added moisture, use a bit of clam broth. Makes six good sized patties.

Submitted by Hazel Woodward, Thomaston, Maine

Spaghetti With Clam Sauce

1 can minced clams, drain and
  reserve juice
1 clove garlic, chopped fine
4 tablespoons olive oil or
  salad oil
1 small can tomato paste
1 large can tomatoes or 4 cups

2 teaspoons oregano
1 teaspoon salt
½ teaspoon pepper
1 pound cooked spaghetti

Saute garlic in oil. Add tomato paste and juice from minced clams, saute 5 more minutes. Add tomatoes that have been strained and put through a sieve so the sauce will be smooth. Then add oregano, salt, pepper and the clams. Simmer until sauce is thickened. Serve over the cooked spaghetti. Serves 6.

Submitted by Mrs. Helen L. Kinner, Brunswick, Maine

Clam And Cheese Canapes

Drain and set aside contents of 1 (7 oz.) can minced clams.
Rub inside surfaces of bowl with cut side of garlic clove.
Cream thoroughly in bowl:

1 package (3 oz.) cream
  cheese, softened
2 teaspoons lemon juice
¼ teaspoon salt
¼ teaspoon monosodium
  glutamate

⅛ teaspoon pepper
5 drops Tabasco sauce
Blend in minced clams

Spread on canape bases. Garnish with slivers of pimento,
ripe olives and stuffed olives.

Submitted by Evelyn Dunton, Rockland, Maine

Clam Fritters

2 eggs
1⅛ cups minced clams (3
  7-ounce cans), drained
½ tablespoon clam juice
¾ cup cracker crumbs

2 teaspoons finely minced onion
½ teaspoon salt
Dash of pepper
2 tablespoons shortening

Beat eggs, add drained clams, clam juice, cracker crumbs,
onion, salt and pepper and mix well. Melt about 2 tablespoons
shortening in a hot, heavy frying pan. Drop in spoonfuls of the
mixture, patting them into cakes. Fry 3-4 minutes or until brown.
Do not cook too long as it makes the clams tough.

Submitted by Mrs. Edward Kiskila, Friendship, Maine

Clam Scallop

40 salted crackers
1 tablespoon butter
2 eggs
3 cups milk

½ teaspoon salt
1 teaspoon minced onion
2 cans minced clams with juice

Roll crackers into crumbs and reserve ⅓ cup with the butter
for top.

Beat eggs, add to the milk with salt and onion. Stir in clams
with juice. Pour into buttered casserole, cover with crumbs and
butter. Bake 1 hour at 350 degrees.

Submitted by Julia Burgess, Waldoboro, Maine

Scalloped Clams

1 can minced clams, water and all
1 cup of salted crackers, crunched

1 egg, beaten
1 cup milk
¼ cup melted butter
Salt and pepper to taste

Mix altogether and let stand ½ hour. Put in casserole, bake 45 minutes in 350 degree oven.

Submitted by Margaret G. Hoyt, Houlton, Maine

Crabbies For Canapes

1 stick butter or margarine
1 jar Old English cheese spread
1½ teaspoons salad dressing or mayonnaise

½ teaspoon garlic salt
½ teaspoon seasoned salt
1 can (7 oz.) crabmeat
6 English muffins

Let cheese and butter soften to room temperature. Mix with salad dressing and salts. Add the crabmeat. Spread on split end of muffins and freeze. Cut into 4 or 6 pieces, broil until bubbly crisp.

Submitted by Myrtle Achorn, Waldoboro, Maine

Crab Delight

1 large can evaporated milk
1 pint sweet milk
½ cup flour
1 tablespoon butter
2 eggs well beaten
¼ pound strong cheese, grated
1 teaspoon salt

½ pound cooked flaked haddock
(Optional — can use 2 cans crabmeat)
Crushed corn flakes
1 can crabmeat (can use fresh or frozen)

Make a cream sauce with the milks, flour, butter and salt. When sauce is thickened, add grated cheese, crabmeat and well-beaten eggs. Place in a buttered casserole and top with crushed corn flakes, bread crumbs, or any topping you like. Bake 30 minutes in a 350 degree oven.

Submitted by Doris W. Pratt, Castine, Maine

Seafood Supreme

1 can frozen shrimp soup
1 can minced clams
  (undrained)
2 tablespoons Chinese brown
  gravy sauce

½ pound fish or ¼ pound
  shrimp
2 packages Chinese frozen
  peapods

Heat the shrimp soup with minced clams and other seafood. (Scallops, crabmeat or lobster may be used in place of fish or shrimp.) Heat in double boiler for 20 minutes. Then add peapods and brown gravy sauce. Simmer for 10 minutes longer. Serve over Chinese noodles, rice or regular noodles.

Submitted by Elsie Groth, Waldoboro, Maine

Seafood Casserole

1 can crabmeat
1 can shrimp
1 cup mayonnaise
⅛ teaspoon pepper
1 cup chopped celery

1 onion, chopped
1 teaspoon Worcestershire
  sauce
½ teaspoon salt
Buttered bread crumbs

Mix all ingredients except bread crumbs together. Put in a greased casserole. Top with the buttered bread crumbs. Bake at 350 degrees for 45 minutes.

Submitted by Ms. M. K. Rollins, Abbot Village, Maine

Seafood Casserole

1 can crabmeat
1 can shrimp
1 cup mayonnaise
Dash of pepper
1 cup chopped celery

1 onion chopped
1 teaspoon Worcestershire
sauce
½ teaspoon salt
Buttered bread crumbs

Toss crabmeat and shrimp with mayonnaise, add dash of pepper, celery, onion, Worcestershire and salt. Put into a greased 1½-quart casserole. Top with buttered crumbs. Bake at 350 degrees for 45 minutes.

Submitted by Ms. M. K. Rollins, Abbot Village, Maine

Seafood Casserole

1 can crabmeat (can use fresh)
1 can shrimp (can use fresh)
1 cup celery, cut up
½ medium onion
½ green pepper
2 tablespoons butter
1 teaspoon Worcestershire sauce

1 cup mayonnaise
Bread crumbs or crushed
potato chips
(Can use a small can
mushrooms instead of
or with celery.)

Saute the onion and green pepper in butter. Mix with the rest of the ingredients and pour into a greased casserole. Cover with crumbs or crushed potato chips. Bake at 350 degrees for 25 to 30 minutes.

Submitted by Mrs. Austin W. Miller, Friendship, Maine

Seafood Casserole

2 cans frozen cream of
shrimp soup
2 tablespoons butter
¼ teaspoon paprika
½ teaspoon salt

½ cup cream
1 can crabmeat
1 can lobster
2 tablespoons flour
Buttered bread crumbs

Melt butter and blend in the 2 tablespoons flour; add soup, paprika, salt and cream in the top of the double boiler. Pick over the seafood and add to the mixture in the double boiler. Mix well. When hot, pour into a buttered casserole and cover with buttered bread crumbs. This mixture may also be served in patty shells without the addition of crumbs.

Submitted by Julia Cogswell, Fort Fairfield, Maine

151

Seafood Casserole

2 tablespoons butter
2 tablespoons flour
2 cans frozen cream of shrimp
  soup
¼ teaspoon paprika
¼ cup cream
1 can (6½ oz.) crabmeat

1 can (6½ oz.) shrimp,
  deveined
1 can (6½ oz.) lobster
  or meat of 1 lobster
Buttered crumbs

Melt butter in top of double boiler over hot water, blend in flour, add soup, paprika and cream. Pick over seafood (to remove any bits of shell) and add to double boiler. Mix well and when hot pour into buttered casserole. Cover with buttered bread crumbs. Bake in moderate oven 350 degrees for 25-30 minutes or until mixture is hot and bubbly. This may also be served in patty shells without the addition of crumbs.

Submitted by Peg Smith, Newport, Maine

Mock Lobster Pie

1 can crabmeat
1 can shrimp
1 cup celery, cut up
1 cup mayonnaise

2 or 3 tablespoons margarine,
  melted
½ package dry stuffing

Partially cook the celery, then mix it with the crabmeat, shrimp and mayonnaise. Put in a shallow type casserole. (I use a whole pint of Maine shrimp, fresh or frozen when I have it.)

Blend melted margarine with the stuffing and put on top of the fish mixture. Bake in 300 to 325 degree oven 30 minutes or until brown.

Submitted by Hazel Hills, Warren, Maine

Crabmeat And Cheese Broiler Sandwiches

1 7-oz. can of crabmeat
1 8-oz. package processed
  cheese

1 stick butter or oleo
6 hamburg rolls or English
  Muffins cut in half

Melt cheese and butter in top of double boiler. Remove spines from crabmeat and add to mixture. Spread on 12 halved rolls. Place under broiler for 3 to 5 minutes or until bubbly and slightly brown.

Submitted by Mrs. Elbert (Betty) Stallard, Hingham, Massachusetts

SALMON SALAD BOWL, perfect choice for hot summer days.
(Recipe on Page 154)

Escalloped Crab And Oysters

2 cans crabmeat, flaked
(about 3 cups)
3 cups oysters
1 cup butter

½ cup flour
2 cups rich milk
2 cups fine crumbs

Divide the butter. In ½ cup butter saute the crumbs until they are brown. Melt ½ cup in double boiler and away from the fire add the flour and seasoning to taste. Blend and slowly add the milk. Stir over hot water until thick and smooth. Oil a casserole and arrange layers of cream sauce, crab, oysters, and crumbs. Top with crumbs. Bake about ½ hour at 350 degrees. Serves 6-8.

Submitted by Grace Perkins, Bangor, Maine

Salmon Balls

1 can salmon, shredded fine
2 eggs, well beaten
3 or 4 tablespoons sweet cream

2 tablespoons flour
⅛ teaspoon baking powder
¼ teaspoon salt

Mix salt with flour and baking powder. Stir into the beaten eggs with the cream. Stir in shredded salmon. Drop by spoonfuls into hot fat and fry brown.

Picked this one up in Canada. Good!

Submitted by Loana S. Shibles, Palmyra, Maine

Salmon Salad Bowl

1 pound can salmon
½ cup French dressing
Lettuce leaves

Cucumber slices
Tomato wedges
Radish roses

Drain salmon and flake into large pieces. Pour French dressing over the salmon and chill for several hours. Line a large salad bowl with lettuce torn into bite-size pieces. Heap chilled salmon into center and surround with cucumber slices, tomato wedges and radish roses. Serve without tossing the salad. Pass mayonnaise or French dressing. Serves three or four.

Submitted by Mrs. Rita M. Grindle, South Penobscot, Maine

Broccoli And Salmon Casserole

1 package cooked frozen
  broccoli
1 can salmon, flaked and
  bones removed
1 No. 2 can tomatoes,
  drained

Cheese sauce
Buttered bread crumbs
2 hard cooked eggs

Place the cooked broccoli in the bottom of a casserole. Place the canned salmon in the next layer, the drained canned tomatoes next. Pour cheese sauce over the contents and sprinkle buttered crumbs over the top. Heat through in a 350 degree oven. Garnish with the hard-cooked eggs, sliced or quartered. Serves 6.

Cheese Sauce
Melt 5 ounces of processed American cheese in the top of a double boiler. Stir in ¼ cup of milk or the juice from the tomatoes.
Submitted by Elizabeth G. Wiers, St. Albans, Maine

Baked Salmon Cakes

1 envelope instant mashed
  potato (5 servings)
1 egg, slightly beaten
¼ cup finely chopped celery

1 tablespoon minced onion
1 pound can salmon
1 tablespoon butter, melted
Cornmeal

Prepare mashed potatoes according to directions on package, but reduce water to 1¼ cups. Cool slightly. Stir in egg, celery and onion. Gently fold in the salmon which has been drained and broken up. Grease generously 12 muffin cups, dust with cornmeal. Spoon salmon mixture into cups, drizzle with melted butter and sprinkle with cornmeal. Bake in a hot oven (400 degrees) for 20 minutes. Serve with cheese sauce.

Cheese Sauce
In a small saucepan combine ⅓ cup of milk, ¼ cup mayonnaise and 4 slices of American cheese (grated), heat just to simmering to melt cheese. Stir occasionally.
Submitted by Mrs. Ruth Savage, Palmyra, Maine

Salmon Cakes

2 cans salmon (1 pound each), drained, boned and minced
3 tablespoons lemon juice
2 teaspoons onion powder or 1 medium onion, minced
¼ teaspoon pepper
½ teaspoon salt (preferably, seasoned salt)
¾ cup mayonnaise
2 eggs slightly beaten
3 cups bread crumbs
1 cup cornmeal
Oil for frying

Mix together salmon, lemon juice, onion, salt, pepper, mayonnaise, eggs and bread crumbs. Shape into patties and roll in cornmeal. Refrigerate 1 hour or more. When ready to use, heat oil in skillet over medium heat and cook patties until brown on each side. Serves 4-6.

Submitted by Eleanor C. Linton, Ca. den, Maine

Salmon Casserole

1 can pink salmon (1 pound size)
1 teaspoon lemon juice
3 cups milk
6 cups corn flakes
Season with salt and pepper to taste

Remove bones from the salmon and sprinkle with lemon juice. Add milk and cornflakes (mixture should be soupy), season to taste. Turn into a buttered casserole dish, set in a pan of hot water and bake at 350 degrees until firm. Serve plain or with an egg or cream sauce. This is tasty, quick and easy.

Submitted by Isabel T. Howard, Dover-Foxcroft, Maine

Salmon Casserole

1 cup bread crumbs
1 cup milk
1 cup crumbled salmon (de-boned)
1 egg
Pepper and salt
Cracker crumbs

Heat together the bread crumbs and milk. Mix salmon with egg, salt and pepper. Combine with bread and milk and put all in a casserole; sprinkle top heavily with cracker crumbs. Bake approximately ½ hour at 350 degrees. Serves 2.

Submitted by Josephine C. Philbrick, Camden, Maine

Salmon Chowder

1 can salmon (1 pound size)
1 cup cooked tomatoes
1 small onion, finely sliced
2 cups water

¼ cup flour
3 cups milk
½ teaspoon salt or to taste.
Dash pepper

Flake salmon, add tomatoes, onion and water. Simmer 20 minutes. Combine flour, milk and seasonings, cook until thickened, stirring constantly. Add the salmon mixture and serve at once. Serves 6.

Submitted by Mrs. Gloria Matthews Simmons, Rockland, Maine

Potato And Salmon Chowder

4 cups diced raw potato
1 cup diced carrots
3 cups water
1 tablespoon salt (or salt to suit taste)
1 package frozen peas
⅓ cup butter

⅓ cup chopped onion
¼ cup flour
5 cups milk
1 pound can salmon, flaked
1 cup chopped celery
½ teaspoon Worcestershire sauce

Put potatoes, carrots, water and salt into a saucepan, bring to a boil, lower heat and simmer until vegetables are tender, about 15 minutes. Add peas and boil 5 minutes more. Remove from heat. Saute onion in butter in a skillet until tender. Add flour and stir until smooth. Cook for 1 minute, and add 2½ cups milk, stirring constantly over low heat until mixture is thickened. Add salmon with liquid to the vegetables. Add the white sauce, celery, Worcestershire sauce and remaining milk. Reheat before serving. Serves 8.

Submitted by Mrs. Ernest Mitchell, Guilford, Maine

Golden Salmon Chowder

3 cups sliced carrots
1 medium-sized onion, sliced
½ cup chopped green pepper
½ teaspoon salt
4 cups water
2 tablespoons all purpose flour
1 and ⅔ cups evaporated milk (undiluted)

2 cans salmon (7¾ oz. each) drained
1 teaspoon garlic salt
1 teaspoon celery salt
¼ cup chopped parsley (optional)
¼ teaspoon thyme

continued

Combine carrots, onion, green pepper, water and salt. Cook until vegetables are tender. Make a paste of the flour and a little of the milk and add to the mixture, then add the rest of the milk. Add salmon and seasonings. Cover and cook for 10 minutes. Serve hot.

This recipe came from Kent, Washington, during the days of the Gold Rush.

Submitted by Mrs. Eugene Murphy, Mt. Desert, Maine

Quick 'n Easy Salmon Patties

1 can salmon	½ cup flour
1 egg	1½ teaspoons baking powder
⅓ cup minced onion	1½ cups shortening or oil

Drain salmon and save 2 tablespoons of the liquid. In a medium bowl mix salmon, egg and onion, until sticky. Stir in the flour. Add baking powder to salmon liquid and stir into the salmon mixture. Form into small patties and fry until golden brown about 5 minutes in hot oil or shortening. Serve with tartar sauce or your favorite salad dressing.

Submitted by Mrs. Austin W. Miller, Friendship, Maine

Salmon Patties

1 can (1 pound) pink salmon	½ cup flour
1 egg	1½ teaspoons baking powder
⅓ cup minced onion	1½ cups shortening

Drain the salmon and save 2 tablespoons of the liquid. In a medium mixing bowl mix the salmon with the egg and onion until sticky. Stir in the flour. Add baking powder to the salmon liquid and stir into the salmon mixture. Form into small patties and fry until golden brown (about 5 minutes) in hot shortening. Serve with tartar sauce.

Submitted by Mrs. Rita M. Grindle, South Penobscot, Maine

Salmon Jolly

1 teaspoon butter	4 cups canned salmon (2 lbs.)
½ teaspoon salt	1 can condensed cream of
Dash pepper	mushroom soup
2 medium onions, sliced in	½ can water
rings	

Melt butter in a baking dish. Break salmon into bite-size flakes. Spread half the salmon in the baking dish, sprinkle with salt and pepper and scatter half of the onion rings over top. Add remaining salmon and onion rings. Dilute mushroom soup with the ½ can of water and pour over all. Bake 20 minutes in a 400 degree oven. Serves 6.

Submitted by Margaret Jenny, Belgrade, Maine

Salmon Loaf

2 eggs
1 (1 lb.) can salmon
3 slices soft bread cut in
 small cubes

1 teaspoon salt
¼ cup butter or margarine,
 melted
1½ cups milk

Break eggs in bowl and beat until light. Drain salmon, remove skin and bones, flake. Add to eggs with bread cubes, salt and butter. Heat milk to lukewarm and add to first mixture. Mix throughly. Put in greased 7x3x2½" loaf pan. Bake in a 350 degree oven for 1 hour.

Submitted by Eva Meservey, Jefferson, Maine

Salmon Loaf

1 small can salmon
1 tablespoon melted butter
Salt and pepper
½ cup bread crumbs

½ cup milk
1 tablespoon lemon juice
2 eggs

Mix all ingredients thoroughly and pack into a baking dish. Set in a pan of hot water, and bake for 30 minutes at 350 degrees.

Submitted by Clara W. Thornton, North Haven, Maine

Baked Salmon Loaf

1½ cups milk
1 slice bread (I use more)
4 tablespoons butter

2 cups canned salmon or 1 can
2 eggs, beaten
½ teaspoon salt

Heat milk, bread and butter in double boiler until creamy. Remove the bones from the salmon. Mix the salmon with the beaten eggs and salt then stir into the milk, bread and butter. Stir well. Bake in greased pan 1 hour at 350 degrees.

Submitted by Corinne W. Small, Damariscotta, Maine

CLAM AND CHEESE CANAPES. The mixture may be served on a variety of crackers and breads or on tomato aspic slices for a buffet. (Recipe on Page 149)

Salmon Loaf

2 eggs, well beaten
1 cup cracker crumbs
½ cup milk

Salt and pepper to taste
2 tablespoons butter, melted
1 large can red salmon

Mix all together and pour into loaf pan. Bake at 350 degrees for ¾ hour.

Submitted by Martha Wilson, Thomaston, Maine

Salmon Loaf

2 cups cooked cream of wheat
1 can of salmon

2 eggs
Salt and pepper

Beat eggs and mix with salmon and cream of wheat. Season with salt and pepper. Bake in a greased bread tin about 40 minutes at 350 degrees. Serve with egg sauce and garnish with parsley.

Submitted by Carrie S. Libby, Palmyra, Maine

Salmon Loaf

1 can salmon, mashed fine
½ cup cracker crumbs
½ teaspoon salt
¼ teaspoon pepper

½ teaspoon lemon juice
½ cup hot milk
3 egg yolks, beaten
3 egg whites, beaten stiffly

Mix cracker crumbs with salt, pepper, lemon juice and hot milk. Combine with mashed salmon. Add to this the beaten egg yolks and last add the stiffly beaten egg whites. Bake in a 350 degree oven for approximately 45 minutes. Time varies as to size of pan used.

Submitted by Annie Rogers, Jefferson, Maine

Escalloped Salmon

One can of salmon finely broken, the skin and bones removed, 3 cups of cracker crumbs. Arrange in layers in baking dish. Sprinkle with salt and pepper. Add bits of butter. Cover with milk that has been mixed with the liquor from can and bake.

Submitted by Myrtle MacLauchlan, Ripley, Maine

Ring of Plenty

2 cups hot cooked rice
1½ cups hot cooked peas
1 medium onion, chopped fine
2 tablespoons melted margarine
1 can mushroom soup
Salt and pepper
1 large can of salmon, drain
   and reserve juice

1½ cups buttered salted
   cheese crackers
or
Plain crackers with ¼ cup
   grated cheese blended in

Blend together the rice, peas, onion, margarine, soup and reserved salmon juice. Season to taste with salt and pepper. Flake the salmon and blend into the mixture. Generously butter a 2-quart casserole and also butter the outside of a large custard cup or 303 size empty can. Place cup or can in the center of the casserole and half fill can with hot water. Place the salmon mixture in casserole around center dish and cover with cracker crumbs. Bake in a 350 degree oven for 30 minutes. Remove the center dish carefully and fill center with hot seasoned carrots or whole kernel corn.

This may be baked in casserole without center dish and vegetables served on the side. I keep a 303 size can on hand to use in center of casserole.

Submitted by Mary Sprowl, Liberty, Maine

Trudy's Supper Salad

1½ cups cooked rice
¾ cup mayonnaise
1 can salmon or tuna fish
3 tablespoons green pepper
2 tablespoons chopped onion
Olives

⅓ cup chopped celery
2 tablespoons lemon juice
2 hard cooked eggs, sliced
3 medium tomatoes cut in
   wedges

Flake salmon or tuna fish carefully. Blend other ingredients, except tomato wedges, eggs and olives. Toss lightly. Add salmon or tuna fish, mixing gently just enough to blend in. Arrange on crisp lettuce, garnish with the olives, tomato wedges and eggs. This is a very tasty and marvelous fish salad.

Submitted by Mrs. Gertrude C. Cyr, Old Town, Maine

Fish Souffle

1 can salmon, flaked or 1
  pound of any cooked fish
1 cup bread or cracker crumbs
2 cups milk

Salt and pepper to taste
Juice of 1 lemon
3 egg yolks, lightly beaten
3 egg whites, stiffly beaten

Soak the bread or cracker crumbs in milk, add salmon. Season with salt, pepper and lemon juice. Then add the lightly beaten yolks of the eggs. Fold in last the stiffly beaten whites. Put in greased casserole and bake in a moderate oven 25 minutes. Serve with creamed or mashed potatoes. Delicious.

Submitted by Mrs. Gertrude C. Cyr, Old Town, Maine

Salmon Loaf Souffle

1 can (1 pound) salmon
½ teaspoon salt
¼ teaspoon paprika
¼ teaspoon pepper
2 tablespoons lemon juice

½ cup cracker crumbs
3 beaten egg yolks
½ cup hot milk
3 egg whites, beaten stiff

Combine salmon with salt, paprika, pepper, lemon juice, cracker crumbs, egg yolks, and hot milk. Lastly fold in the stiffly beaten egg whites. Pour into a baking dish and bake at 400 degrees for ½ hour.

Submitted by Isabel T. Howard, Dover-Foxcroft, Maine

Salmon And Vegetable Pie

3 tablespoons oleo or butter
3 tablespoons flour
½ teaspoon salt
¼ teaspoon pepper
1½ cups milk
1 pound can salmon

1 cup green peas, cooked
1 cup diced carrots, cooked
1½ cups fluffy mashed potato
Melted butter
Paprika

Prepare a white sauce with butter, flour, salt, pepper and milk. In a baking dish arrange alternate layers of salmon, peas, carrots and white sauce until all ingredients have been used. Mash and season the potato and pile on top of the fish and vegetables. Brush with melted butter and sprinkle with paprika. Bake in a hot oven 400 degrees until brown and heated through, about 35 minutes.

Submitted by Mrs. Ernest Mitchell, Guilford, Maine

Down-East Roll-Ups
Sardines
(For the appetizer tray)

1 can (4 oz.) Maine sardines
6 hard-cooked egg yolks
1 cup cooked rice
2 tablespoons grated onion
Salt and pepper to taste

2 teaspoons prepared mustard
Dash of Tabasco sauce
2 tablespoons mayonnaise
12 slices bacon, cut in halves, crosswise

Mash the sardines and egg yolks. Add rice and onions; season with salt and pepper and mix to blend. Add mustard, Tabasco and mayonnaise. Stir the mixture and spread on bacon slices. Roll and fasten with wooden picks. Place on a rack on a shallow baking pan and bake in a hot oven 450 degrees F for 15 to 18 minutes, or until the bacon is crisp. Serve hot.

Submitted by Mrs. W. E. Schrumpf, Orono, Maine

Sandwich Spreads
Sardine Spread

1 can sardines
2 tablespoons chopped stuffed olives

1 teaspoon lemon juice
Mayonnaise to moisten

Sardine Filling

Blend 1 medium can sardines with 1 (3 oz.) package cream cheese and light cream enough to moisten.

A 1974 high school graduate, Stevie Wiers makes these sandwiches for the family lunch — uses his own imagination.

Submitted by Stephen Wiers, St. Albans, Maine

Sardines On Lemon Toast

1 can sardines
⅛ teaspoon paprika
Salt to taste
Grated rind of 1 lemon

1 tablespoon lemon juice
¼ cup butter
1 teaspoon prepared mustard
Toast

Saute sardines in own oil, season with paprika and salt, set aside. Cream lemon rind, lemon juice and butter, add the mustard. Spread over the toast and lay sardines on top.

Submitted by Olga Burkett, Thomaston, Maine

SARDINES ON LEMON TOAST. These Maine-canned fish are
tops on toasted or plain breads. (Recipe on Page 164)

Individual Maine Sardine Pizzas

3 cans (4 ounces each)
  Maine sardines
6 hamburger buns
2 tablespoons butter or
  margarine

¾ cup catsup
1 tablespoon chopped onion
¾ teaspoon oregano
Dash garlic powder
½ cup grated cheese

Drain sardines. Break into large pieces. Split rolls and spread butter on each half. Place rolls, butter side up, on a cooky sheet, 15x12 inches. Distribute sardines equally on each half roll. Combine catsup, onion, oregano, and garlic powder. Place approximately 1 tablespoon catsup mixture over sardines. Sprinkle cheese on top. Bake in a very hot oven, 450 degrees, for 8 to 10 minutes or until cheese melts and rolls toast. Serve hot. Serves 6.
From National Marine Fisheries Service, Chicago, Ill.

Shrimp Delight

1 medium onion, minced
2 tablespoons margarine
1 cup thin cream or milk
1 can tomato soup
⅛ teaspoon soda

½ teaspoon Tabasco sauce or
  dash paprika
1 cup cooked minute rice
1 can of shrimp, cut coarsely
  (can use fresh shrimp)

Combine all ingredients and cook in double boiler until thickened. Serve on crackers. One may add more shrimp to the amount above or double the recipe.
Submitted by Mrs. E. Ashley Walter, Jr., Waldoboro, Maine

Shrimp Casserole

Butter
Green pepper
Large onion
3 tablespoons flour
4 large canned tomatoes

1 cup tomato juice
3 cans shrimp
Salt and pepper to taste
Tabasco sauce to taste
Rice

Melt a good sized piece of butter, add green pepper, coarsely chopped and onion. Cook until soft. Add flour and cook until thickened. Add tomatoes and tomato juice and simmer, now add the shrimp and seasonings. Serve on cooked rice.

Submitted by Gladys Philbrick, Rockland, Maine

Rice And Shrimp Casserole

1 can cream of celery soup
1½ cups water
Grated onion to taste
1 cup uncooked minute rice

1 can shrimp
1 package frozen peas
¼ pound grated cheese

Heat together the soup, water and onion. Put half of this mixture in a greased casserole, next add the rice, shrimp and frozen peas. Now add the remaining half of soup mixture and spread the grated cheese over top. Bake ½ hour in a 350 degree oven.

Submitted by Mrs. Austin W. Miller, Friendship, Maine

Cheese Shrimp Custard

7 slices of bread
Butter or margarine
½ pound cheese
2 small cans of shrimp

3 eggs, beaten
2½ cups milk
½ teaspoon salt
½ teaspoon paprika

Remove crusts from the bread, spread with butter or margarine. Cut bread into cubes. Slice cheese and in a greased casserole alternate bread, cheese and shrimp. Beat eggs with milk, salt and paprika. Pour over the mixture in the casserole. Bake for 1 hour in a 350 degree oven. (May want to use less salt or use fresh shrimp.)

Submitted by Mrs. E. Ashley Walter, Jr., Waldoboro, Maine

Seafood Chowder

1 cup chopped onion
½ cup chopped green pepper
1 clove garlic, crushed
2 tablespoons cooking oil
1 can (15 oz.) tomato sauce
¼ cup rice (uncooked)
1 can (4 oz.) shrimp

2 cans (7 oz.) tuna
1 teaspoon salt
1 bay leaf
¼ teaspoon thyme
Dash cayenne
1 quart of hot water.

continued

Saute onion, green pepper and garlic in oil until tender. Add rice, tomato sauce, salt, bay leaf, thyme, cayenne and water. Simmer until rice is cooked. Add shrimp and tuna. Simmer for 15 minutes more. Makes 4 generous servings. (Serve hot.)

Submitted by Mrs. Ernest Mitchell, Guilford, Maine

Shrimp Manicotti

¼ cup chopped onion
2 tablespoons olive oil
1 large can tomatoes
1 can tomato paste (6 oz.)
1 tablespoon basil
1 teaspoon salt
¼ teaspoon black pepper
1 bay leaf

2 cans (5 oz.) shrimp, chopped
½ pound ricotta or small curd cottage cheese
1 garlic clove
8 ounces manicotti or broad noodles
½ cup grated Parmesan cheese

Saute onion in oil, add tomatoes, tomato paste, basil, salt, pepper and bay leaf. Simmer 1½ hours until very thick. Combine shrimp with the cottage cheese and garlic and refrigerate at least one hour to blend flavor. Cook manicotti. Stuff loosely with shrimp mixture and arrange in greased 2-quart casserole. Pour tomato sauce over the top. Sprinkle with cheese. Bake at 350 degrees 25 to 30 minutes.

Submitted by Mrs. Dolores Reglin, Orrington, Maine

Seafood Newburg

2 cans shrimp (5 oz.)
3 cans tuna, flaked (6½ oz.)
1 can crabmeat (6½ oz.)
1 can mushrooms (3 oz.), sliced
Sherry (optional), ¼ cup
½ cup shortening

¾ cup flour
½ teaspoon salt
4 cups milk
2 teaspoons Worcestershire sauce
6 eggs, hard cooked

Combine fish, mushrooms and sherry. Melt shortening and stir in flour and salt. Add milk and Worcestershire sauce, stirring constantly until thickened. Combine with fish mixture and place in a 12"x8"x2" baking dish which has been rubbed with shortening. Bake in moderate oven at 350 degrees about 30 minutes. Serve over hot toast or biscuits and top with hard cooked egg quarters. Crackers may be used also. Serves 12.

Submitted by Ivis M. Fowle, Newport, Maine

Maine Newburg

2 cans of newburg sauce with shrimp and sherry
2 cans of tiny Maine shrimp
    or
½ pound frozen shrimp

1 box frozen peas (cook by directions)
Thin toasted buttered bread
    or
Fine buttered crumbs

Mix in a double boiler the newburg sauce, shrimp and peas. Heat well and serve over slices of thin buttered bread, toasted.

This can be combined in advance and turned into a casserole. Top with fine buttered crumbs, set in a pan of hot water and heat in the oven. Serve over rice.

Submitted by Florence V. Jackson, New Vineyard, Maine

Mackerel Stew

1 can mackerel
1 can peas
4 cups milk

Butter
Salt

Heat mackerel in saucepan over low heat. Add drained peas. Add milk and heat. Add butter and salt to taste. Serve hot.

Submitted by Mrs. Evelyn C. Roberts, Damariscotta, Maine

Tuna Casserole

2 cups elbow macaroni
1 (7 oz.) can tuna
1 green pepper, chopped
1 small can mushrooms
½ teaspoon salt

⅛ teaspoon pepper
4 tablespoons butter
4 tablespoons flour
3 cups milk
4 ounces American cheese

continued

Cook macaroni in salted water and drain. In buttered casserole combine macaroni, tuna, green pepper and mushrooms. Add salt and pepper. Prepare a sauce of butter, flour and milk. Add cheese and stir to melt. Pour sauce over the ingredients in casserole and bake in a slow oven 325 degrees for 40 minutes or until the dish bubbles.

Submitted by Mrs. Dolores Reglin, Orrington, Maine

Tuna Casserole

1 can shoestring potatoes
1 can tuna (any size)
⅔ cup milk

3-ounce can mushrooms, drained
¼ cup pimentos

Take 1 cup of the potatoes and combine with tuna, milk, mushrooms and pimentos. Put into a casserole dish and add remainder of potatoes on top. Bake at 375 degrees for 20 minutes.

Submitted by Nellie Ifemey, Thomaston, Maine

Tuna Casserole

1 can tuna fish
1 can cream of mushroom soup
  (undiluted)

Potato chips, crushed

Combine tuna fish with mushroom soup. Place in baking dish and put the potato chips on top. Bake, until bubbles up and is heated through.

Submitted by Elizabeth H. French, Auburn, Maine

Tuna Fish Casserole

1 package noodles
1 can tuna
1 can mushroom soup

½ cup milk
Potato chips, crushed

Cook noodles. Mix together the tuna, soup and milk. Add to noodles and put in a casserole. Put crushed potato chips over top and heat in oven.

Submitted by Eva Meservey, Jefferson, Maine

Tuna And Broccoli Casserole

1 package frozen broccoli
1 can tuna, flaked
1 can mushroom soup
½ can milk
½ cup potato chips

Cook broccoli for 3 minutes. Drain, place in baking dish and cover with flaked tuna. Add soup, milk and chips. Bake at 450 degrees for 15 minutes.

Submitted by Eleanor Clark, Thomaston, Maine

Tuna-Rice Casserole

½ cup milk
1 cup water
1 (10½ oz.) can condensed cream of mushroom soup
1 (7 oz.) can tuna
½ cup grated Cheddar cheese
½ teaspoon dry mustard
½ teaspoon salt
1½ cups minute rice
1 (16 oz.) can green peas or green beans, drained
¼ cup dry bread crumbs or crushed potato chips
2 tablespoons butter, melted

(As a substitute for the peas and beans, can use a 10-ounce package of 5-minute sweet green peas or a 9-ounce package of 5-minute cut green beans.)

Blend milk and water into soup in a greased 1½ quart casserole. Stir in tuna, cheese, dry mustard, salt, rice and vegetable. Combine bread crumbs and butter. Sprinkle over top of casserole. Bake at 400 degrees for 25 minutes. Makes 5 servings.

Submitted by Corinne W. Small, Damariscotta, Maine

Tuna Mushroom Casserole

1 can mushroom soup
1 can tuna (solid white)
½ cup mayonnaise
1 small can sliced mushrooms (drained)
1 cup chopped celery
1 package frozen mixed vegetables, cooked and drained
Buttered crumbs

Mix first 6 ingredients together in a casserole, top with the buttered crumbs. Bake at 375 degrees for about 30 minutes or until all bubbly.

Submitted by Mrs. Austin W. Miller, Friendship, Maine

171

Tuna And Mushroom Casserole

1 can cream of mushroom soup
1 small package potato chips

1 can tuna
¼ cup milk or cream

Make crumbs of the chips, but not too fine. Combine ¾ of them with the soup, milk and tuna. DO NOT ADD SALT. Spoon into a buttered casserole. Top with remaining chips. Bake at 350 degrees 30 minutes.

Submitted by Ruth A. Savage, Palmyra, Maine

Tuna Macaroni Casserole

1½ cups cooked macaroni
1 can tuna chunks
1 can cream of celery soup

½ cup milk
Cheese slices

Place macaroni in a greased casserole. Add tuna, soup and milk. Arrange cheese slices over top. Bake 30 minutes in a 350 degree oven.

Submitted by Ruth Bond, Jefferson, Maine

Five Can Casserole

1 can tuna
1 can chicken noodle soup
1 can cream of mushroom soup

1 can Chinese noodles
1 small can evaporated milk

Mix all together and bake in a 350 degree oven about ½ hour.

Submitted by Eleanor Clark, Thomaston, Maine

Tuna-Rice Casserole

½ cup milk
1 cup water
1 can cream of mushroom
  soup
1 can tuna
½ cup grated cheese

½ teaspoon dry mustard
½ teaspoon salt
1½ cups cooked rice
1 can green peas
¼ cup crushed potato chips

Blend milk, water and soup and put into a greased casserole. Stir in tuna, cheese, mustard, salt, rice and peas. Sprinkle crushed chips over top or can use buttered crumbs. Bake at 400 degrees for 25 minutes.

Submitted by Ruth Bond, Jefferson, Maine

Tuna And Vegetable Casserole

6 hard cooked eggs, quartered
1 package frozen peas
1 can tuna
1 can asparagus, drained
3 tablespoons butter

5 tablespoons flour
Salt and pepper
2 cups milk
Buttered crumbs
Cheese (optional)

Place eggs in casserole, top with peas, then tuna, then asparagus. Make a white sauce with the butter, flour, salt, pepper, and milk. Pour over vegetables. Top with buttered crumbs. Can add some cheese. Bake at 325 degrees for 40 minutes.

Submitted by Eleanor Clark, Thomaston, Maine

Tuna Treat

1 can (6½ oz.) tuna fish
2 cups frozen peas
1 can cream of mushroom soup
⅓ cup milk

4 eggs, separated
¼ cup Cheddar cheese, grated

Mix together the first four ingredients and bake in a 2-quart casserole for 10 minutes at 400 degrees. Meanwhile, beat yolks of eggs until lemon colored and fold in the Cheddar cheese. Beat whites of eggs until stiff and fold into the yolk mixture. Take casserole from oven and spread egg mixture over the baked tuna and cook for 20 minutes more at 400 degrees. Serve with tossed salad, melba toast or potato chips and a simple dessert.

Submitted by Mrs. Carl Otto, Orono, Maine

Easy Tuna Casserole

1½ cups cooked noodles
1 (6½ oz.) can tuna
1 (10 oz.) can cream of mushroom soup

½ cup evaporated milk
1 cup grated cheese
½ cup chopped onion
Potato chips, crushed

Combine first 6 ingredients, place in 9 x 9 inch baking dish. Top with the potato chips. Bake at 450 degrees for 20 minutes.

Submitted by Isabel T. Howard, Dover-Foxcroft, Maine

Tuna Rolls

1 can tuna (large)
3 hard boiled eggs, cut up
1 cup cheese, cut up
1 tablespoon green pepper, chopped
2 tablespoons onion, chopped

2 tablespoons olives, chopped
2 tablespoons pickle relish
½ cup mayonnaise
8 hotdog rolls

continued

Mix the first 8 ingredients together and fill the hotdog rolls, wrap in foil. Place in 250 degree oven for 35 minutes or until cheese has melted. Can be served hot or cold.

Submitted by Mrs. Robert Dutil, Lisbon Falls, Maine

Canned Tuna

Steam tuna until cooked. Chill 6 to 12 hours. Cut into jar-length pieces. Pack into hot pint jars leaving 1 inch head space. Add 1 tablespoon salt and 2 tablespoons salad oil to each pint. Adjust caps. Process 1 hour and 30 minutes at 10 pounds pressure.

Submitted by Stella Brooks, Bath, Maine

New England Tuna Chowder

1½ cups diced raw potatoes	¼ cup chopped onion
Salt and pepper to taste	1 can tuna (6¼-7 oz.)
¼ cup chopped bacon or salt pork	4 cups milk

Cook potatoes 15 minutes or until tender, add salt and pepper. Fry bacon or pork until lightly brown, add onions and cook until tender. Add to potatoes, also tuna and milk. Heat to serving temperature.

Submitted by Ruth A. Savage, Palmyra, Maine

Tuna Fondue

5 slices bread	3 eggs
1 can tuna (7 oz.)	2 cups milk
¼ pound (½ cup) American cheese, grated	1 teaspoon salt

Place the bread as is in the bottom of a 1½-quart baking dish, or crusts may be trimmed off and the bread cubed. Flake the tuna and spread over bread. Sprinkle grated cheese over the tuna. Beat together eggs, milk and salt. Pour over the tuna mixture. If crusts are left on the bread, use about ¼ cup more milk. Bake in a 325 degree oven for one hour or until knife inserted comes out clean. Serve with mushroom sauce if desired.

Submitted by Becky Wiers, St. Albans, Maine

Chopstick Tuna

1 can cream of mushroom soup	1 cup celery, sliced
¼ cup water	½ cup salted toasted cashews
1 can tuna	
1 can (3 oz.) chow mein noodles	¼ cup onion, chopped.

Combine soup and water. Add 1 cup chow mein noodles, tuna, celery, cashews and onion. Toss lightly. Place in ungreased 10 x 6 x 1½ inch baking dish. Sprinkle remaining noodles over top. Bake at 375 degrees for 15 minutes or until heated through. Garnish with mandarin orange sections. Yields 5-6 servings.

Submitted by Charlotte C. Hopkins, Rockland, Maine

Tuna Fish Delight

1 can tuna fish	4 large potatoes, boiled
1 can mushroom soup	Butter
1 can cream of celery soup	Paprika

Drain tuna fish. Mix the two soups together. Slice potatoes and put a layer in bottom of buttered casserole, then some tuna fish and top with some of the soup mixture. Repeat the layers with potatoes on top. Dot with butter and sprinkle with paprika. Bake at 400 degrees 40 minutes. Serves 6.

Submitted by Mrs. Dolores Reglin, Orrington, Maine

Tunaburgers

1 can tuna, drained and flaked	⅓ cup mayonnaise
½ cup fine fresh bread crumbs (2 slices)	2 tablespoons chili sauce
½ cup chopped celery	1 teaspoon lemon juice
2 tablespoons minced onions	4 hamburger buns, toasted

Combine first 4 ingredients. Blend next 3 ingredients and stir into tuna mixture. Form into 4 patties. Fry in lightly oiled skillet over medium heat about 5 minutes or until browned. Serve on hamburger buns with lettuce and sliced tomatoes. Serves 4.

Submitted by Mrs. Hazel Beal, Waterboro, Maine

Tuna Pie

1 can tuna	½ teaspoon onion salt
½ cup Swiss cheese	½ teaspoon celery salt
3 eggs, beaten	Pimento
1 cup milk	Paprika
Dash of pepper	1 unbaked 9" pie crust

continued

Flake tuna and distribute evenly in the pie crust, dot with Swiss cheese. Beat the eggs, add milk, pepper and the two salts. Pour this over the tuna and cheese, add bits of pimento and sprinkle paprika over the top. Bake in hot oven 15 minutes than reduce heat to moderate and bake about 30 minutes longer.

Submitted by Maud Feyler, Rockland, Maine

Tuna Hot Dogs

1 can tuna fish
1 green pepper, chopped
1 small onion, chopped
½ cup grated American cheese

2 teaspoons Worcestershire sauce
1 tablespoon prepared mustard
Enough mayonnaise to mix

Mix all these ingredients together. Fill hot dog rolls. Wrap in aluminum foil. Place on cookie sheets. Bake for 40 minutes in 350 degree oven.

Submitted by Mrs. Hazel Beal, Waterboro, Maine

Gold Fish Salad

1 package orange gelatin
1 can mandarin oranges
1 can (7 oz.) tuna fish
2 tablespoons lemon juice
Paprika
2 tablespoons vinegar

¾ cup finely chopped celery
1 teaspoon finely chopped onion
Salt and pepper to taste
1 tablespoon salad dressing
Salad greens
Lemon wedges

Prepare gelatin according to directions on package except use ¼ cup less water. Set aside to cool. Rinse a mold (fish if you have one) with cold water. Then arrange in mold the orange sections. Mix the tuna fish with the lemon juice, lay on top of orange sections and sprinkle with paprika. Add the vinegar to the orange gelatin and pour over the tuna and orange sections until just covered. Chill and when set, add the remainder of orange gelatin to which has been added the celery, onion, salt, pepper and salad dressing. Chill and unmold, garnish with salad greens and lemon wedges.

Submitted by Mrs. Stella Brooks, Bath, Maine

Pinky's Tuna Fish Salad

2 (7 oz.) cans tuna
1 cup chopped onions
1 cup chopped celery
¼ cup diced green pepper

2 cups bean sprouts
¾ cup mayonnaise
2 tablespoons soy sauce
Lettuce

Break up the tuna and toss gently with onions, celery, green pepper and bean sprouts (if using canned sprouts, drain them). Mix mayonnaise and soy sauce and fold into the salad. Serve on lettuce. 6 servings.

Submitted by Gwen Church Ellis, Warren, Maine

Danish Fish Salad

1 can (8 oz.) tuna fish
1 cup canned peas
1 cup cold boiled spaghetti

2 tablespoons vinegar
½ sliced red pepper or sliced pimento

Mix all together and serve with lettuce and mayonnaise. Serves 6.

Submitted by Leota Cuthbertson, Rockland, Maine

Spaghetti And Tuna

4 tablespoons oil
1 onion, chopped
1 can tomatoes, strained
Few sprigs parsley, chopped
1 clove garlic, chopped

Salt and pepper to taste
1 can tuna
1 pound spaghetti
2 ounces grated cheese

Pour oil into saucepan, add chopped onion. Cook until brown then add the strained tomatoes and cook slowly for about ½ hour. Add parsley, garlic, salt and pepper. In a bowl flake the tuna and add to the tomato sauce, cook five more minutes. Set aside. Cook the spaghetti in rapidly salted boiling water for about 10 minutes or until tender. Drain and arrange on a hot platter. Season with sauce and sprinkle with the grated cheese. Serves 6.

Submitted by Pam DiNapoli, Waldoboro, Maine

Tuna Fish Pie

6 medium potatoes, sliced
⅛ pound salt pork
Salt and pepper
1 small onion

1 large can tuna
4 teaspoons margarine or butter

continued

SPAGHETTI AND TUNA, a new combination for this versatile fish. (Recipe on Page 177)

Cook potatoes in water to cover, add salt and pepper. Fry onion in sliced pork and add to potatoes. Place in buttered dish a layer of potatoes, then a layer of tuna. Add remaining butter. Cover with rich biscuit dough or pie crust and bake until potatoes are done when tested with a fork.

Submitted by Athelene Hilt, Union, Maine

Crusty Tuna Pie

2 cups cubed potato
2 cups sliced carrots
½ cup chopped onion
1 can tuna (7 oz.)
1 teaspoon salt

⅛ teaspoon pepper
1 can cream of chicken soup
1¼ cups water
Buttered bread

Cook vegetables until done. Drain, combine with tuna, salt and pepper. Mix soup with water and pour into a casserole. Place slices of buttered bread cut in fourths on top. Bake until brown.

Submitted by Eleanor Clark, Thomaston, Maine

Fish Loaf

2 cans tuna (7 oz. cans)
1½ cups dry bread crumbs
½ teaspoon celery salt
½ teaspoon salt

Dash of pepper
1 tablespoon chopped onion
1 egg, beaten
1 cup milk

Mix together the fish, bread crumbs, 2 salts, pepper and onion. Add beaten egg to the milk and combine with the fish mixture. Place in a greased loaf pan. Bake at 350 degrees for about 30 minutes until brown. Makes 4 to 6 servings. (2 cups cooked fish can be substituted.)

Submitted by Corinne W. Small, Damariscotta, Maine

Tuna Sandwiches

1 large can tuna, drained
1 tablespoon minced onion

1 tablespoon minced celery
1 tablespoon minced carrot

Combine tuna, onion, celery, carrot and enough mayonnaise to mix smooth with electric mixer, then add the noodles. This is especially good with a little watercress on small tea sandwiches.

Submitted by Bodine Ames, Vinalhaven, Maine

Sandwich Fillings
Tuna Fish

1 large can tuna fish
½ cup chopped celery
½ cup chopped, stuffed
  olives
½ cup salad dressing

Mayonnaise
½ cup chow mein noodles,
  crushed

Blend all ingredients together. You may add 1 hard-cooked egg to the mixture if you wish.

Tuna Spread

Flake 1 small can of tuna fish; combine with ¼ teaspoon salt, dash Tabasco and enough mayonnaise to moisten; mix well.

Submitted by Stephen Wiers, St. Albans, Maine

Tuna Fish Patties

1 can tuna (7 oz.)
2 cups mashed potatoes
1 small onion, minced
1 egg

½ teaspoon curry powder
2 tablespoons flour
Salt and pepper to taste
3 tablespoons fat

Combine all ingredients except fat, and mix well. Shape into flat patties and fry in hot fat until browned on both sides. Drain on unglazed paper, makes about 12 patties. Leftover mashed potatoes may be used.

Submitted by Mrs. Stella Brooks, Bath, Maine

Tuna Fish Supreme

2 tablespoons butter, melted
2 tablespoons flour
1 teaspoon salt
1½ cups milk

2 tablespoons mayonnaise
1 cup tuna fish
Bread crumbs or crushed
  cornflakes

Cook butter, flour, salt and milk to make a smooth sauce. Add the mayonnaise. Pour over tuna in deep dish. Cover with the crumbs. Brown in oven.

Submitted by Mrs. Crosby E. Prior, Friendship, Maine

180

INDEX

181